CRACK CIVIL SERVICES IN FIRST ATTEMPT

EASY TO USE TIPS IN PRACTICAL LIFE

DIVEY SETHI

DEDICATED TO

ALL THE CIVIL SERVICES ASPIRANTS

Contents

Foreword

Shri Divey Sethi cleared the UPSC Civil Services Examinations in 2013 and was selected to join the Indian Revenue Service. Based on his own experience and empirical evidence from 7 other successful candidates and several unsuccessful ones, he has prepared a handy guidebook to help other aspirants with Do's and Don'ts. The book flags, very graphically and through bullet points, some practical tips and techniques for success in prelims, optional subjects, and interview.

Despite Sethi's own assertions, it would be an oversimplification to say that his recipe for "smart study" is opposed to "hard work" or that civil services are generally for "mediocrities and average students" only. He accepts that there is no conflict between the pursuit of excellence and a civil service career. Also, on principle, it cannot be disputed that there is no substitute for hard work, and successes achieved through the use of shortcuts or tricks of the trade go only so far and no further. Success achieved through hard work and struggle is more satisfying. Shri Sethi's focus, I would like to believe, is actually only on marrying your hard work with a purposive and result-oriented direction. He would like hard work to be properly strategized and channelized to the targets sought to be achieved. The author presents a concrete step-by-step action plan for preparations for civil service examinations.

The book makes for interesting reading. I am sure it will be widely read, not only by civil services examinees. Although the author considers the coaching industry a menace, it is likely to be the one to derive the maximum benefits from his prescriptions, adopt his tricks of the trade, and reinvent its programs.

I wish the author all success in his civil service career as a revenue officer and thereafter. I hope he will always be motivated by the highest principles of hard work, probity, and public service, above narrow aims of personal success and aspirations. I wish he continues to wield his pen and produce more books.

– Subhash C. Kashyap

Foreword

The Civil Services Examination is not only one of the most prestigious exams in India but is also considered to be among the toughest to clear all over the world. In this context, the book in your hand, CRACK CIVIL SERVICES IN FIRST ATTEMPT, assumes significant importance. The book has dwelled on pragmatic strategies, rather than inspirational and motivational text, to emerge successful in the Civil Services Examination. The author has also put forth the concerns of various sections of the aspirants regarding the present pattern of the preliminary examination.

The chapters have been profoundly placed in a logical sequence, which every aspirant will appreciate while reading this book. The text that needs to be read has been detailed minutely but explicitly, attracting immediate attention to the tables and the charts. The book elucidates to an aspirant the reasons for taking the decision to study for Civil Services Examination through various stages of the exam: preliminary, mains, and interview. It plunges into the in-depth analysis of the psychology of the aspirants and their insecurities, which have been explained through the means of myths and FAQs at the end of each chapter.

The book in your hand is also a wake-up call to the unfettered profit-making coaching sector in this field of Civil Services Examination preparations. The author has rightly commented on the big coaching institutes and their unchecked drive to create profit at any cost. Their role in the lives of aspirants, and also in shaping the minds of future administrators, must be called into a wider public debate. The sarcasm and humor make the book an engrossing read for all.

I wish Divey Sethi all the very best and hope that the book fulfills its desired objective for the aspirants.

Blessings and wishes,

– Dr Kiran Bedi, IPS

Preface to the Fourth Edition

Almost a decade into the civil services now, after getting selected as an IRS officer of the 2014 batch, it is the right time for me to revise the book and publish the current fourth edition. I am a mid-career bureaucrat now and, fortunately for me, at a juncture in life where I can find time to devote to this new edition, a phase of life when you can take the liberty to press the pause button and just ride with the flow of life. It seems that life has come to the intermission/interval, analogous to it being compared to watching a movie in a theater. The anxiety of performing, constantly seeking validation and appreciation for your work, continuously competing with other bureaucrats in different dimensions of life, burning the midnight oil to learn the work to overcome challenges that existed during the initial years of the services, the need to be a perfectionist in every aspect of life, and the awkwardness associated with 'not-knowing' have, miraculously, disappeared from within myself completely. What remains is the pursuit of excellence, a radical openness to new experiences, a desire for minutely observing learnings that life has to offer, and a profound sense of contributing to the greater good of society.

It is with this new lens that I sit to pen down the evolutionary process of UPSC Civil services preparations, identifying the problems, the pitfalls, and the traps, and how to foresee them and transcend them, or at the very least, how to navigate through these in the least damaging manner. This book will not only delve into the evolving pattern of Civil Services Examination based on a data-driven approach but will also focus on discerning fundamental characteristics and qualities that should exist for cracking the toughest entrance examination in India and, subsequently, how to imbibe these indispensable qualities as an aspirant to significantly increase the chances of your success at the Civil Services Examination. This is not a book that talks about success, making money in life, how to be happy in life, and after beating about the bush of 'that one factor of success, 'ends up saying that it is only determination, perseverance, or as a matter of fact, the power of the subconscious mind to manifest into reality that can make one successful!' Instead of this, what has been presented in this book is a step-by-step strategy that helps you realize your potential to the fullest– through internalizing some changes inside of you and complementing it with the strategy to study smartly – and this helps you reach the zenith of your preparations so that the chances of your success increase considerably.

I also advise the aspirants not to mistake this book as some magical wand to clear civil services. This book, at the most, can be categorized as a self-help book particularly designed for the needs of civil services aspirants so that the probability of your success at cracking the exam increases significantly. As Shri Subhash C. Kashyap has rightly put in his foreword to the previous editions of this book, whenever I have used smart work, as opposed to hard work, it "actually means marrying your hard work with purposive and result-oriented studies, and hard work needs to be properly strategized and channelized to the targets sought to be achieved." This edition of Crack Civil Services, in the first attempt, apart from dealing with the aspect of targeted study answering your questions of why, when, where, and how, deliberates further into changes you are required to make internally that would equip you with capabilities necessary to study smartly, and you would soon realize that this, in fact, is tougher than the actual preparation process.

Lastly, to summarize, I have also elucidated in-depth what you should and should not expect civil services to be. With around a decade of experience as a civil servant and more than a decade as a government servant, previously working as a technocrat through engineering services before becoming an IRS officer, I present to you the current scenario of being a bureaucrat as opposed to not being one, highlighting its stark realities and the alternative career options possible for those who have given up hope after a series of unsuccessful attempts and feel directionless. This is also for those who would love to deliberate very consciously before committing their finite time and energy to civil services preparations.

I have tried to write the book in a lucid and terse manner. Although not possible everywhere to the satisfaction of each aspirant, especially where the complexity of the topics increases, more or less, I have tried to follow the principles of simple brevity, especially in FAQs. The depth of discussion and dialectical approach of knowledge dissemination and proliferation in the manner of FAQs have been increased in most of the chapters. Relevant and appropriate queries of aspirants put forth to me on various social media have been amalgamated in these ever-growing FAQs.

Any person, whether fresher or otherwise, struggling to achieve the desired success in civil services shall find enlightenment by relating to several parts of this handbook. Those who find civil services preparations shrouded behind the clouds of mystery shall find the myth of the enigma melting away as they muster their courage and move in this direction strategically. In fact, anyone, not necessarily an aspirant, slightly curious about civil services and related issues will be elucidated about the concerns surrounding the examination that calls for a wider debate. It is sincere advice that the book should be read in one go, itself, for the very first time, but it has to be reverted to time and again for those specific parts that are of concern or interest to the aspirant.

I express gratitude to all those selected candidates who have contributed to the making of a common strategy, deepest sympathies with those who didn't make it, and still overtly shared the bottlenecks they encountered, and best wishes to those who are still in the process, yet contributed their valuable time to diagnose the reasons for their unsuccessful attempts until now.

Dear aspirant, it is high time that you plan the preparations and then adhere to them throughout this fantastic, mysterious journey of revelations. I hope that you shall read it, imbibe it, follow it, and see your performance increasing day by day, thus increasing the chances of your success in civil services.

– Divey Sethi

PART – I

The Structure v/s The Content

*"Various exams have different contents; how to clear
them is the structure."*

Lately, I have been wondering what core talents or skills I possess, and among a few others, the skill that is insanely imminent is clearing entrance examinations! Starting right from 2003 to 2013, I devoted this whole decade to ace the competitive examinations in India and bagged IIT JEE, AIEEE, CAT, GMAT, GRE, GATE, SSC – Technical, and SSC – CGLE, UPSC IES, and finally UPSC CSE into my kitty of achievements. The only exam I could not clear, despite being absolutely sure of my best attempt toward it, was the CEE (common entrance examination of 2003), which was a gateway to the prestigious Delhi College of Engineering (now Delhi Technical University). From the year 2010 onwards, I ended up clearing 5 government services examinations from 2011 to 2013, some more than once, the last one being UPSC Civil services. Now that there are no more exams left to clear, I ponder over, and more so introspect, what the fundamental characteristics of my mind are that helped me crack such a distinguished array of examinations in a span of a decade. Can there be some fundamental traits that my mind followed for every different paper? Can we elicit some common principles that would create apt conditions for the mind of any aspirant to adjust as per the requirements of any entrance competitive examination, irrespective of vastly different patterns? Well, it seems that there are some patterns that my mind followed, though without knowing it consciously, which somehow increased my chances of success at various exams drastically.

These patterns, these fundamental traits or qualities or characteristics, I put as the structure – to be more precise – the structure of mind to learn how to learn & adapt quickly to various diverse patterns of the examination. The subsequent questions of when to study, from where to study, what to study, and how to study are examination-specific issues, which I call the content. The former part, that is, the structure of the mind, is more of a static thing for the broad topic of clearing the competitive examinations, and the latter part, that is, the content, will be dynamic, that is, it shall change as per the needs of a particular competitive examination. To observe the structure of a particular thing, here it is the generalized patterns a mind follows for success at entrance examination, is a tremendous capability, which is a consequence of profound introspection and contemplation developed rigorously through the practice of mindfulness, that is, you go inward looking by watching yourself as a third person and observing minutely for eliciting some common patterns for a particular task at hand. Having said that, I do not expect that you, being an aspirant of UPSC Civil Services, start doing mindfulness introspection and contemplation instead of the task at hand, and that is why I have tried my best to lay bare to the best of my capabilities, the structure we need our minds to resort to for cracking civil services. The first part of the book covers the various aspects, concepts, contexts, and topics of this structure of mind I have referred to. The second part of the book covers the content of the UPSC Civil services, which takes up all the questions related to when, where, what, and how. Upon studying both the parts and going through the process of preparations, you shall realize that part one, which dealt with the structure of the mind required for preparations, is tremendously hard to imbibe and achieve and will show you the sheer power of creating the right structure of the mind to succeed in the entrance examination.

Before I actually delve into the different structures required for the above task, I would like you to further realize, to some extent, the fine demarcation between the structure of the mind and its content through some examples. Let me first tell you that the structure of the mind, in this book, refers to the process of how your mind is thinking and making decisions. It refers to the procedures, checks, and balances your mind is following and why it is following after it has made a decision. On the other hand, the content would refer to what decision has been made and what, how, and when such procedures and checks and balances have been applied after the decision is made. Let us take another example, a very basic one: the structure of the mind of a religious fundamentalist is the same regardless of the religion. Why? Because in all such cases, the mind is locked into the dogma that only a single CORRECT narrative exists for viewing a world. However, that single correct narrative has myriad processes, rules, and procedures accompanying it, which are different for every narrative. Here, we realize that the structure is the thinking process of the mind itself, and the content is what the mind is coming up with during that thinking. Although the above is a very simple example that gives you an idea of how to delineate between structure and content, in reality, the mind comes up with more nuanced distinctions between structure and content. But going through part one of this book, you will slowly realize the sheer power of this when the structure of a mind to clear entrance examination is laid bare in front of you. If it is imbibed into you, then it becomes easy to upload different content that is relevant to the requirements of a particular exam. Let us now begin the journey to discern and enlist some fundamental structures that I have found in myself and what I have not found in those who could not clear civil services, most of them having better knowledge than me, both in-depth and width of the subject.

Grounding in the Present Moment: The Right Mindset

"Perspective about your own self plays a pivotal role in preparations."

While studying for all entrance exams, starting right from IIT JEE to UPSC Civil Services, I noticed that I tend to ground myself subconsciously in the present moment. I have not let the past, which exists only in my memory, and also not the future, which is yet to unfold with time, disturb my preparations. I have not let the achievements or failures of my past entrance examinations or life in general, which now exist in my memories, take over me while studying for Civil Services Examinations. I have also not let the uncertainties associated with clearing the UPSC CSE, which exist in the future, the glamour, the fame, and prestige which I shall receive with success, and the miseries which I shall have to face with failure, take over me while preparing for the examination. In actuality, the past and future don't exist anywhere. In the universe, there is a big eternal now. The past exists only in our memories, and the future exists only in the speculations of our minds. Now, when I look back, I realize that subconsciously, without even knowing, I tend to ground myself in the present moment while doing any work – whether it may be preparations for entrance examinations or any other crucial work as such. It can very well be said that I was "consumed" while preparing for UPSC CSE and any other entrance examination. This I would like to explain with the help of 4 diagrams;

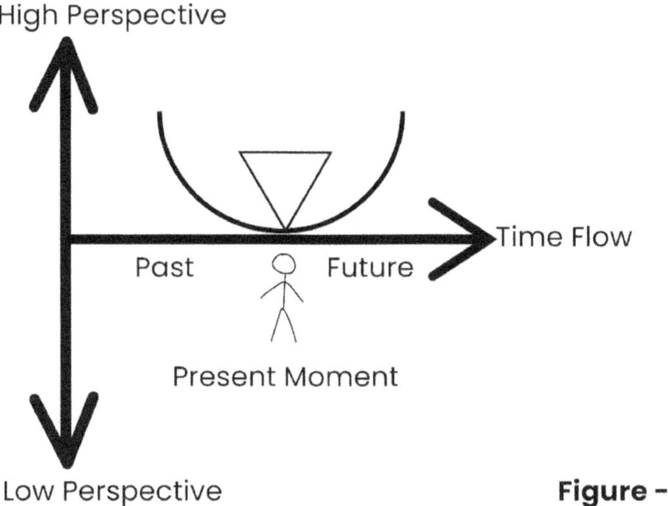

Figure 1: The aspirant has a few successes which he/she remembers or recalls from time to time, along with moving with the arrow of time as the future unfolds. More importantly, he/she thinks positively while grounding himself/herself in the present moment. This is the most positive frame of mind and is reflected by a concave upward shape of perspective both in the past and future.

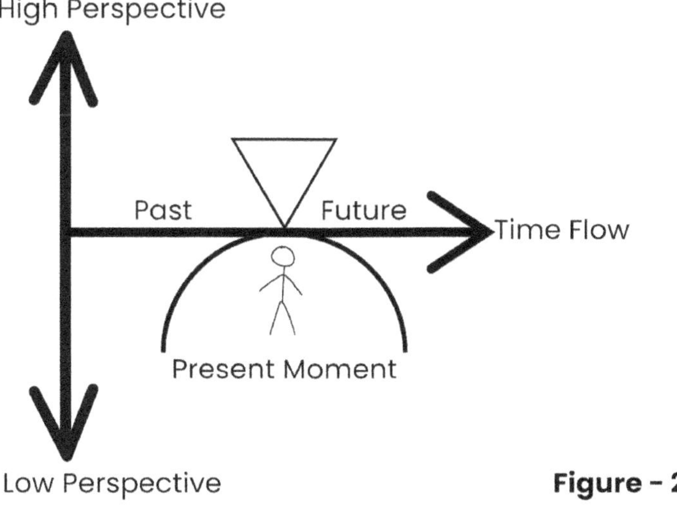

Figure 2: The aspirant has no or very little success in the past and thinks negatively about his/her past, at least in the field of cracking entrance exams and/or studies in general. Apart from that, the aspirant also expects the same to repeat as he/she moves along with the arrow of time when the future unfolds in front of him/her. This is reflected by a convex upwards shape of perspectives both in the past and future. This is the most negative frame of mind and needs to be changed.

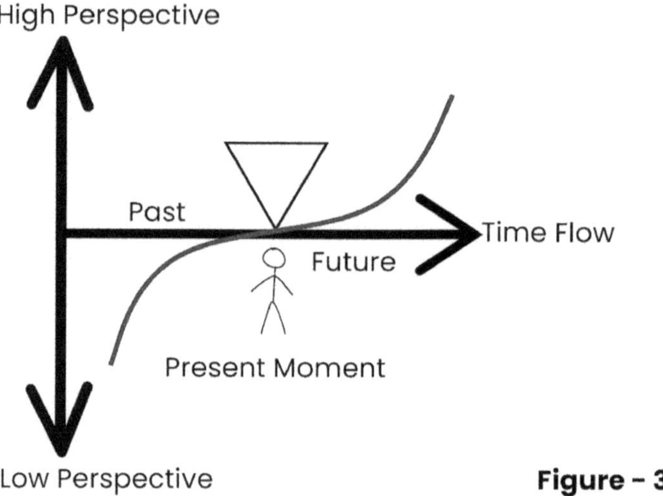

Figure 3: Figure 2 needs to be amended or changed to Figure 3. Here, despite the aspirant having no significant achievements or successes in the field of studies, as indicated by the convex upward curve of the past, the present moment acts as the inflection point. This leads to a concave upward mindset in the future as time unfolds the present moment continuously.

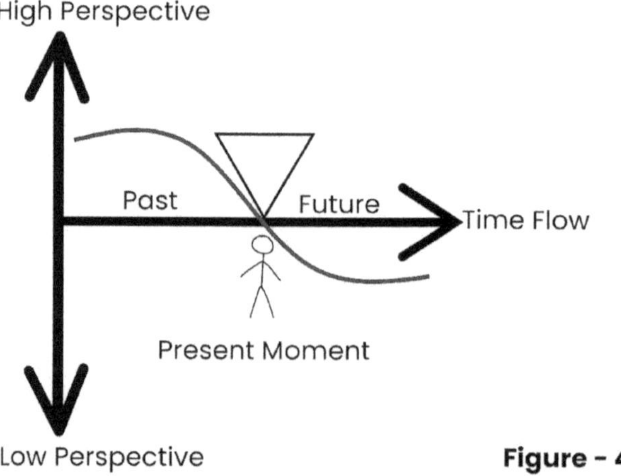

Figure 4: These will be quite rare cases, but because they are rare, they are extremely tough to handle. Why? Here, the aspirant has bagged a few educational achievements in his/her kitty in the past, yet doesn't consider the future to be as bright as the past and, contradictorily, considers the future bleak with the concave upward shape of expectations/perspective while galloping in the present moment. They are suffering from a depressive mindset and, therefore, need to be molded to Figure 1.

Directly going into the preparation of the UPSC Civil services examination without identifying which figure your mindset is in is absolutely not advisable. You should be clear and fully aware of which figure your mindset is in. It will help you address your subsequent preparation. The left portion is generally quite clear by the time you step into the field of CSE Preparations, as the minimum criterion for that is graduation. So either you are through with graduation or have probably completed some years of graduation but have yet to graduate. Nevertheless, you are aware of how you have fared in your studies from schooling, especially after class IX and up until now, whether you have cleared some entrances or not. Therefore, I find that most of the aspirants can very well identify the left part of the aforementioned 4 diagrams, which reflect the past. What is difficult is to evaluate the right part of it – whether you have a positive mindset or a negative mindset while entering into the preparation of the Civil Services Examination.

You will find that very strange; the more you ground yourself in the present moment, the more positive your mindset becomes! When saying the previous sentence, what I mean is how you utilize your present moment, the now that exists, and only that exists actually, because the past is made up of memories and the future is made up of speculations or evaluations, whichever term we may use. The more positive framework of mindset is what you shall get along with it. More importantly, time 'flows' because of the perception of the mind, as the mind only has the function of being nostalgic while digging out the memories of the past and speculating the future, which is yet to occur. Nevertheless, not going into too many nuances of the functionality of the mind, let me limit here to "mindset" and how to change Figure 2 into Figure 3 and Figure 4 into Figure 1, both by grounding yourself in the present moment.

I will give you a live and very simple example. I could only write this book when I grounded myself in the present moment. Although I have a plethora of achievements in the past, if I dwell on the future of whether

I will get the results associated with the book, such as whether I shall get a publisher or not, whether aspirants will like it or not, and so on, the more I became of a Figure 4 mindset. Therefore, after writing the book in 2014, 2015, and 2016, I could not come up with subsequent editions. Apart from having other priorities in life as I aged from a fresher to a mid-career bureaucrat, the aforementioned reason played an important role in not being able to come up with the fourth edition. It was only when I again self-reflected holistically on the entire process of cracking the Civil Services Examination and grounded myself in the present that I could come up with this fourth edition.

Now that you are aware of the fact that grounding yourself in the present moment shall change your mindset and align it with either Figure 1 or Figure 3, which is most important for clearing the Civil Services Examination, the most immediate and natural question is how to ground yourself in the present. The answer is so simple that it evades or goes unnoticed by most minds. The answer is that you should enjoy what you are doing. Think and self-reflect that at times when you are doing any activity that is enjoyable for you; you are most likely grounded in the present. That is, neither the memory of the past haunts you nor makes you feel nostalgic, and neither do the speculations of the future take your attention away. If what you are doing captures your attention, you can very well say that you have grounded yourself in the present moment.

But isn't this a utopian thing I am talking about? That is, how can the studies for Civil Services Examination capture your attention so that you ground yourself in the present moment and subsequent changes in mindset happen? The answer to this question lies in the next chapter.

The Decision to Go for Civil Services: The Why of it

"The ending point is the same as the starting point."

Why did you choose to even appear for civil services? What purpose in your life does the services fulfill? Why do you want to become an IAS/IPS/IRS? All these questions and the like are asked in interviews. These form some basic questions in the interview. Then, the reader may wonder why I am discussing it right at the beginning of this handbook. It is because the starting point is the same as the ending point in this journey. It is also because what you answer in the interview may be very different and even contrary to what your actual reason was for taking to study for civil services! Also, the clarity of the reason for preparing for civil services will help you provide the energy so that you can attend to the mammoth task at hand and, hence, ground in the present moment.

The cause or the inspiration to study for civil services must be known to you. This must not remain in the latent form. I even assure you that there exists a tendency to hide the exact cause, especially when you cannot disclose it in a public forum. You may not disclose it overtly, but you must know it correctly, for it will help you genuinely mold it into some acceptable forms during the evolutionary process of preparations so that you don't have to lie or conceal the reasons at the interview! Let me tell you, dear friends, that those who are sitting in the interview panel of UPSC Civil services are the expert and experienced intelligentsia, and it is not advisable to resort to bluffing techniques, blurring, or hiding facts. Honest presentation of thoughts, that is, authenticity when you speak, is what is required, and that can be done only with the clarity of thoughts. Thus, the interview preparations start from the day you decide to start studying for civil services. The first step is introspecting and discerning the cause of the study and slowly evolving it from a narrower to a much broader and socially acceptable perspective of the purpose of civil services.

For this purpose, I list below various reasons the aspirants choose to go for civil services, some of them my own. From a narrower perspective of the cause to its broader vision, a transformation must take place, for which certain thinking mechanisms are provided, which may be continuously studied and simultaneously imbibed in your personality.

a) **Power:** A candidate successful in his third attempt with a wonderful rank declared his source of inspiration in a public forum, *"When I was a child, I asked my father while walking in front of the district collector's office, 'Who does this office belong to and what is the purpose of this office?' My father replied, 'He is the god in our area, descended from heavens; everything he says is done!'"* I admire that person for overtly announcing the fact that his inspiration to become an IAS officer is power. However, in person, he revealed to me that one cannot be so overt in an interview. Thus, there is no harm in acceptance of the fact that the power that civil services wield motivates one and serves as a cause. Yet, one should transform his/her thoughts to the just use of that power. This is the evolutionary process I am talking about.

   You must have a constant undercurrent of this thought, "Yes! I do strive for power and take up civil services, but vouch for the just use of that power." Dear aspirant, with this thought imbibed in your heart, you shall be true to yourself and aim for the right direction fit for civil services.

b) **Money:** One of the biggest motivating factors, that is, money, finds itself shrouded with irony. It is not there in civil services unless or until astute, unfair means are used to procure it. Civil services promise a decent, above-average living standard. But honest bureaucrats are no match for the 'corporatocrats' as far as the monetary aspect is considered. When I say corporatocrat, I understand the term to mean those who are running the companies at the top level – directors, promoters, hedge fund managers, business families, etc.

So, how do we reconcile the urge to earn money and the hunger for money with civil services? Many people face the same dilemma. Here, we must understand the fact that civil service opens up myriad opportunities in the private sector as well. With 5 or 7 years of experience as a bureaucrat, one can comfortably transition into a senior-level position in the private sector or even start their own venture with the functional experience of administration at hand. At some point, you have to choose between 2 conflicting options!

c) **Unsuccessful/mediocre people:** A lot of aspirants are coming from IITs. These are mainly five – or six-pointers and cannot perform well academically in the highly competitive environment of IITs. Consequently, their placements did not meet their perceived standards.

Once, I asked my friend, a nine-pointer from IIT, who was doing a PhD in the USA, "Why don't you come to India and study for civil services? You can certainly clear it as you are a nine-pointer!" His reply was astonishing, "I have expended all my energies during college life in studies. Now I want to relax a little and enjoy the quality offerings in a developed country." Adding a little humor, he continued, "On the contrary, you are very well positioned to do it. You have surplus energies left, which you saved in your college life and stood as a five-pointer." After we shared a fit of laughter, he continued, "And it gives you a reason and an opportunity to prove your mettle again." Within a week after that conversation, I found myself studying for civil services.

There are many aspirants who have had their share of continuous failures. Some missed IIT and landed up in NIT. Some could not make it into government colleges. Some did not fare well earlier in their adolescence and were awarded arts or commerce out of compulsion. Not all commerce students can go to SRCC, just as not all medical students will get AIIMS. Many, like me, messed up in their college and ended up with poor grades. All these people are there to prove to society that they have the mettle and are important. The Indian education system is such that it provides an opportunity to correct the misdoings of the past. The civil services exam is one such means.

The important thing is that we must acknowledge our failures, mistakes, and wrong decisions, and only then shall we start an endeavor to rectify these.

d) **Dissatisfaction with the present work profile:** It may arise due to diverse issues. People from the I.T. sector generally find themselves imprisoned in front of computers; the monotonous routine further takes a toll. Youngsters in PSUs, mainly in the starting position of management trainee, do not have much liberty to make decisions. The starting job packages in the engineering field are not attractive enough to draw young talent. Teaching, whether in schools, colleges, or coaching institutes, suffers from gender bias and is labeled as a profession of failed individuals. Lawyers face a huge struggle at the beginning of their careers. A middle-class person graduating from college finds it difficult to start a business, both due to a lack of capacity and skills, as well as finances. The interlinking of capacity building, entrepreneurship, funding, and commercialization is weak in the service sector and virtually absent in the production sector. This is exactly what I experienced when I was running a business consultancy for the nationalized banks.

Thus, in this current scenario, civil service finds a connection with the youngsters, and that is why we find the competition increasing every year, reflected by the increasing trend of the cut off in the preliminary examination. It becomes imperative to identify your reason to quit the job and decide to go for the exam.

e) **Vengeance:** One tends to believe that upon clearing the civil services, you may be able to settle your personal equations. I don't know how far this is feasible. But in the worst scenario, even if it is an illusion, an aspirant may continue to believe in it with a promise that he/she won't reveal it until the task is achieved. This unorthodox mechanism can be a source of energy, provided that it is not dissipated by revealing the intent publicly. Slowly, over a period of time, the broader pressing concerns shall be incorporated into the reasons for opting for civil services.

f) **Strategic alliance:** When I was selected in CSE 2013, a close friend of mine, an aspirant himself, came to my house to congratulate me and said, "Mr Sethi, your rate is now at a minimum of one crore." We laughed off at his casual remark. But a profound thought into the matter would make us realize that some aspirants may also get motivated by the possibility of a strategic alliance, a business house, or a political family. If you consider this a factor, then please discern it and accept it; however, you may not reveal it.

g) **Pursuit of excellence:** You may encounter some people who have been continuously proving themselves. Their inspiration is the pursuit of excellence. They will excel wherever they go and will latch onto the best opportunity of that time. Some examples are Jayant Sinha, D. Subbarao, Raghuram Rajan and the likes. Check their career graph, and you will find it. The one I know is a person who hailed from Bihar and stood among the first 5 at the IIT JEE entrance in 2003. During his days at IIT, he was consistently a nine-pointer, and on the second attempt, he secured an All India rank under 5 in civil services as well. This group is rare, and the aspirant must be true to the core if he/she aims to be part of it. If you are motivated by the pursuit of excellence and your past suggests the same, then you will fall into this section.

Further, doing better for you, being career-oriented, and pursuing it simultaneously is not opposed to the goals of civil services. In fact, they must be seen as reinforcing each other.

h) **Broader outlook:** All the above-mentioned personal driving factors have to be shaped into acceptable and socially presentable forms during the course of preparations. This requires a basic understanding of what the goals are for which civil services exist and why. Nation-building and public service are the 2 cornerstones of the civil services.

One must come to terms with the fact that apart from personal endeavors to get through civil services, there is a contribution from society, too, however minuscule it may be. Apart from the immediate contribution of parents, siblings, relatives, and friends, there is a contribution from society which we do not account for or generally ignore. The sweeper that cleans our room, the cook that feeds us if we stay in rented apartments, the rickshaw puller that tows us from our room to the coaching institute, all the teachers right from primary to graduation, the person who throws the newspaper every morning, and so on. Try to recall their faces, step into their shoes, and feel the challenges in their life.

These contributions cannot be ignored. They have to be returned to the society at large. Therefore, the civil services give us the opportunity to serve the people through our decisions, deliberations, enforcement of policies, etc. The reach of civil services is wide, and so is the responsibility. Just imagine the plight of our fellow men if civil services personnel are incompetent, motivated only by private accomplishments, or lacking the basic ethos of civil services. It is this tendency that we shall shed from our personality during the study period and not one week before the interview!

Thus, as I said, the private pursuits and personal agenda must be clearly realized and discerned. Generally, there may not be one single personal cause for taking to study for civil services, and it may be a combination of 2 or 3 existing together. Once the exact root cause/s is/are surfaced, the task is not yet finished. Now, the goal is to accommodate that narrow personal cause into a broader view of civil services, and that will take time. It will surely but slowly happen as we progress in the preparation, only with the full knowledge that this transformation can't be accomplished in a single night. And thus, I may correctly say that the preparation for the interview starts right from the idea of studying for civil services!

❖ **The Motivational Theory:**

Apart from discerning the reason and the way of taking to prepare for civil services, one must also answer another question. How do you see yourself in the bureaucracy? Is it just another job for you? Or do you see civil services as a career or passion? Or maybe you are inspired by the idea of being a part of civil services in the country?

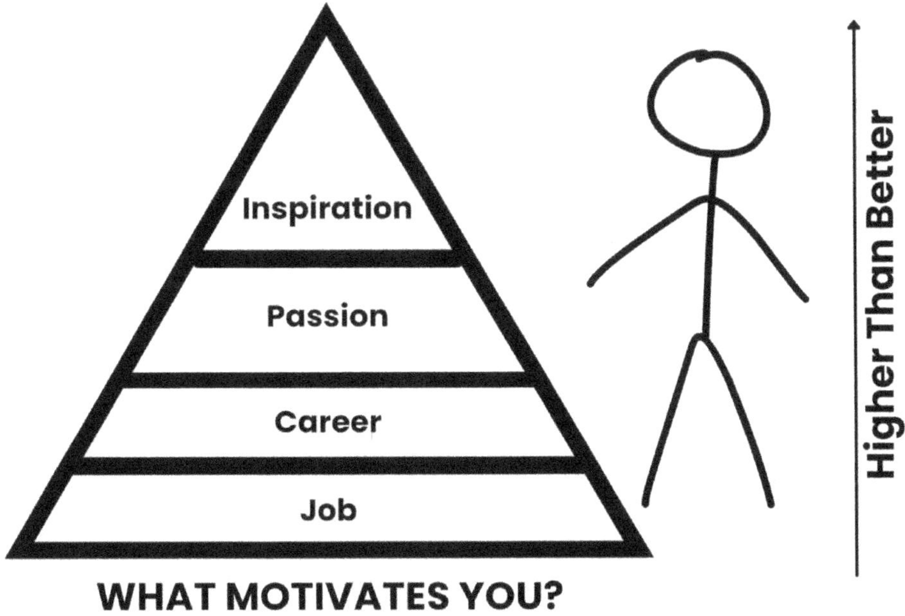

If you are studying for civil services because you don't find anything else to do, then try not to be an aspirant. A right aspirant is one who sees civil services at least as a career, if not a passion. If you take to preparations assuming that civil services are just another job, then you could possibly be in for a big surprise. It is not just 'another' job, such as working in an MNC at the starting level, as compared to working as a civil servant at the starting level. The massive reach and intensity of the impact of decisions you make as a civil servant are far greater than those of similar positions in other jobs. Therefore, you should take to the preparations of civil services at least as a career of 30 – 35 years, and you would be doing this in the next around 30 years of your life, which is half of your functional life. You would run into difficulties if you started your preparations journey thinking civil services are just another job and are actually not passionate about it. The biggest challenge is that you cannot lie because the assessment of your motivation is not to be done by anyone else but you. So there is no scope for lying, only deluding yourself into believing that you are passionate about civil service or that you find it is a good career option when, in fact, you think it to be just a mere job.

Consciously Deciding to Study:
The When of it

"Nothing else to do but studying is not the same as studying and doing nothing else."

There is no particular "right time" to start preparations for UPSC Civil Services. One can start even during college as an undergraduate at one end and can even begin preparations after a decade of completing college if the need arises, of course, due to several reasons. The more important aspect is how you define the fact that you have commenced preparing for the Civil Services Examination. In my opinion, the preparation starts right from the time you are even "consciously thinking" of starting your preparations because it is, or it should be, effectively addressing the question of why civil services should be your career. There is also a remarkable difference between 2 kinds of aspirants: one who starts preparing because he/she has nothing else to do and the other who takes up preparations and does nothing but prepare. The former starts preparing aimlessly without knowing the reasons why he or she has taken up the task. This kind of variety enrolls in the coaching institute not for guidance but mostly for falling in line or a need to be disciplined by an external 'magical wand' of the institute. How the coaching exploits you for having that 'magical wand' is a very interesting part of the complete story of UPSC Civil Services preparations, and details are found in the subsequent dedicated chapter on this.

But, for now, dear aspirants, take into account and let it settle subtly in your mind that there is a profound difference between starting preparation because you've got nothing else to do and doing nothing but preparing. The former may also become an aspirant of civil services because it is trendy! Saying, "I am studying for UPSC Civil services," is and has always remained in vogue and probably buys a person at least one or 2 years, mostly after graduation, before finally giving up and surrendering what was initially not his/her cup of tea, only because of a casual or rather unconscious attitude toward life. The latter, on the other hand, is more conscious of his or her decision to start studying for civil services, and that creates enough motivation for doing nothing but preparing.

However, yet the aspirants would want to know when to start the actual preparations. When I refer to actual preparations, I do not merely refer to the idea of preparing for CSE subtly forming in your mind so as to decipher the reasons for studying, but now I refer to the actual and exact baby steps you would take in this direction, such as taking books, notes, or probably deciding upon joining a coaching or even taking a decision of not to join any coaching. The question is more important, especially for those prospective aspirants who have found the charms of civil services irresistible right in their college days. I am referring to those aspirants who are in the process of graduation but have made up their minds to plunge into the preparations.

Two schools of thought exist here. The former, which I refer to as the idealists, find the blood rushing into veins upon the very mention of such words or similar to these by college-going students, "I am trying to make up my mind to give civil services." Or maybe, "How about a career in civil services? Is it worth it?" The idealists have all the guns loaded for their long list of how-tos, do's and don'ts, and whatnot!

I take the liberty to narrate an incident or, rather, an encounter with one of my distant relatives who had been at a prestigious post of chairmanship of an institution of national importance. I somehow landed up at his house upon severe persuasion from my parents to discuss the present dismal state of my grades at college and what could have been done to circumvent the disaster of being stranded as an unemployable graduate after a few months! After briefing the unconvincing reasons for my gloomy track record in college, I mistakenly uttered the word, "Uncle, I also thought about civil services and....." He cut me here and, with a glitter in his eyes, started off, "Oh yes. That's the best option. You start right from tomorrow. But remember, you have to read 2 newspapers each day. Also, by the time you complete the last year of college, you must have completed each NCERT from 6th to 12th class so that fundamentals are laid down. Simultaneously, listen to the news on FM or watch Rajya Sabha and D.D. news. Oh! Before I forget, you have to start practicing the past years' GS questions in writing and show me some of your answers after one month."

"I was right! It is indeed not my cup of tea," I murmured to my mother sitting beside me and softly slipped out of their house and never came again. Now I refer to this as the latent power of the idealists – they would burden the soul with a heavy weight of preparations, and this may induce a fear and flight response from the prospective or a would-be aspirant of civil services.

Now, let us tackle the scenario with the pragmatic school of thought, which I generally advocate to most college-going students who wish to prepare for CSE in the near future. I truly believe that college life, from where you attain your first degree, forms one of the best phases of your life and should be cherished and enjoyed in a healthy manner. These are a few carefree days of your otherwise stressed lives that must be devoted to different but equally important tasks – tasks that won't overburden you or deviate from your immediate priority, that is, graduating with the best possible score in the prescribed time period for the degree undertaken. These tasks will form an additional armory to tackle the war of CSE later on. Some of these important tasks are;

1. **Analyze and compare various career options:** Your job brings satisfaction only if you like the work you do. The job profile should be such that you enjoy your work. The rest – money,

power, responsibility, and respect – are bound to come if one does his/her work with commitment and dedication. Thus, while choosing civil services as a career option and plunging into the preparation, one must evaluate the options he/she has while graduating from college. Look at the kind of jobs offered by companies during placements and compare it with the prospects of higher education. You should come up with convincing answers to the questions as to why you should not go for higher education – maybe an MBA or specialization in your field of expertise. Why don't you intend to get a job through campus placement?

2. **Cultivate your interests:** College years are some of the most formative years of one's life and career. It is a phase of life when one has the liberty of taking time to introspect and discover definitive interests. These interests may be developed into hobbies and nurtured. This will not only help in interviews for CSE or any other exam but, more importantly, provide a new dimension to your personality. You never know, in this uncertain life, when your interest or hobby may turn into a full-time passion and become a major source of earnings!

3. **Reading:** It is one such act which I recommend with all force. I realize and accept that it is difficult for students to spend their 'precious' time, which they could otherwise put to a myriad number of 'usages' such as gossiping, watching TV, Facebooking, Instagramming, WhatsApp, etc. But this is an activity that will build the foundation of whatever you do after your college years. Reading is an exercise that will develop your capability to concentrate and focus on one topic, countering several distractions that hit your mind simultaneously. And one must agree that the power of concentration is required to excel in any field of work. The added benefit to the activity is developing a powerful vocabulary, which will give you confidence in both written and oral communication.

College-going students should do justice to themselves by taking up at least these 3 tasks mentioned above, apart from the course curriculum they have to study. This would prepare them for the future battle, whether it is a job, higher studies, or civil services.

Leverage the Power of the Not-Knowing Mode

"Most significant moves in life are very counter-intuitive in nature."

Have you ever wondered what the interview panel of UPSC Civil services wants from a candidate? One of the strongest misconceptions is that bureaucrats "know" everything under the sun! The reality is very far from it. You cannot know everything, and the interview panel acknowledges and accepts this truth. They are looking for someone who, apart from other qualities, has an acceptance of this very fact that you can't know everything and your knowledge is limited, and someone who is humble enough to accept this, provided that he/she is willing to learn the unknown.

Most of the significant moves in life are very counter-intuitive, just like playing chess; a grandmaster would sacrifice a noteworthy piece under his or her kitty, which would look like a mistake to a person with myopic vision, only to realize later on that this was a trap created by the grandmaster so as to checkmate the opponent. Here, I am asking you to become a grandmaster by setting up a default not-knowing mode in your mind with respect to UPSC Civil services, which, in fact, is very counter-intuitive from the perspective of an ordinary aspirant. Most of the aspirants are preparing in the default knowing mode and are not only very opinionated about anything and everything you throw at them but also rarely acknowledge that there is a limit to the human mind as far as knowing is concerned, specifically with respect to the general nature of the examination syllabus.

I am also not here to give you fake assurances regarding your sense of epistemology, that is, the way you inculcate what to know and what not to know. Your entire understanding of knowledge may be incorrect and, therefore, the outcomes. I am here to challenge your entire approach to how you begin understanding anything about the study of UPSC Civil services, correct, whether it means dismantling these fragile foundations you have constructed for your comfort in the mere fact that you are studying civil services. Do not solely find solace in the fact that you are merely studying for civil services but in whether you have true mastery over the subjects you have studied or not.

Have you ever mindfully watched yourself in a manner that a third person would see over every aspect of your life? Most probably, the answer to this question would be a big NO. This power to shift perspectives is very rare and is generally available and accessible as the consciousness level of a person increases. I am proposing a very counter-intuitive thing in this chapter, which is to be mostly in a not-knowing mode rather than a knowing mode. During this last decade, I have known many varieties of aspirants: those who were aspirants and stayed as aspirants, as they remained unsuccessful at every attempt of UPSC, and those who made it into the final list. Also, a few of such aspirants left civil services and preferred other employment opportunities, and finally, those aspirants who could not be settled till now after tremendously failing at each and every attempt of UPSC. One thing I am definite about those who made it to the final list is that they were more modest than the others who didn't find a seat. They were more comfortable with not knowing a particular thing, and there was, in fact, a listening ear for openness to learning rather than the awkwardness, essentially accompanied by the not-knowing mode.

By now, you should have observed that the not-knowing mode would have an effect on making you humble toward knowing more than before. It's almost a decade since I have been working as a mid-career bureaucrat now, but I never felt awkward or obstinate when it comes to a particular task at hand of which I am not aware. I would humbly accept my lack of knowledge in that particular task only to develop a listening ear to learn it from any other source if it is important enough.

Here, I also narrate an incident that I was fortunate enough to oversee. Very recently, I visited Rajendra Place in New Delhi, a hub of civil services preparations, where most coaching institutes are located. While having tea at one of the stalls, I found 2 aspirants initially talking about the relevance of voting in a democracy. One of the aspirants hailed from Bihar and could not go there to cast his vote in the Lok Sabha election of 2024. On this, he was pulled right and left by the other aspirant who hailed from Shimla, Himachal Pradesh, and who, in fact, took the pains of going there and casting the vote. The discussions ranged from how even one vote could make a difference to the results to chastising those who, due to some reason or the other, could not contribute to the massive feast managed by our election commission in India. The discussion between those 2 turned from a battle of opinions to verbal abuse to the extent that several other people had to intervene to calm them and hold their horses.

The incident above I narrate to make a point that there is no fruitfulness in any discussion, which is so opinionated that the thin boundary between discussing and fighting goes away. In any case, my dear aspirants, we should learn to be silent. Only if we are silent are we able to develop a listening ear, which is more important for the task at hand, that is, clearing the Civil Services Examination. Speak only when required, if required at all. In the aforesaid example, one of many others that you may have observed with yourself and others, where the content may be different, but the structure of discussion remains more or less the same, the election commission & political parties take into account the fact that there will be some voters who would not be able to vote due to myriad reasons.

The crux of many such scenarios is to observe silence and save your life energies so that you can develop a listening ear, and only then, the power of not-knowing can be leveraged to the best.

General Traps, Myths and Frequently Asked Questions

A) I have been an average or below-average student throughout my career. Can I crack civil services?

Dear aspirant, I must tell you that this civil services exam is primarily for academically average students but with common sense. One who has maintained an average performance throughout their career has a good chance of clearing this exam. In fact, I was an average student throughout my school life and slightly below average in arts subjects. Furthermore, I graduated with a GPA of 5. Therefore, I believe that when a person who has performed averagely or even below average in their career so far decides with determination to shed this tag of mediocrity, the chances of passing the exam become significant.

B) Do the people from IITs, IIMs, SRCC, JNU, AIIMS, Maulana, etc., have better chances in civil services?

In recent times, we have seen a lot of engineers and doctors clearing civil services, especially those who are from institutes of national importance and international fame. However, the question can be reframed as to why these aspirants perform well. It is the pressure of keeping up with the expectations of society that helps them perform well. One of my friends from IIT failed in the preliminary in his second attempt. Reflecting on the course of events, he candidly said, "I am ashamed as it is not expected of an IITian to fail in the preliminary." What is this? It is the pressure of expectation from the immediate society that helps these people put in the last mile effort. But here is the catch. During the course of preparations, one must forget that he/she has a legacy of successful graduation; otherwise, I have seen stalwarts becoming complacent and ending up with nothing in their hands, even after 4 attempts.

C) I am not from IIT, IIM, SRCC, AIIMS, etc. Do I have a chance? How do I start?

Now, if that external pressure is missing owing to your college not being 'reputed enough' and thus the people from that college or institute are expected to remain mediocre throughout their life, then the internal pressure of expectation has to be created. All those aspirants who are not from IITs, IIMs, AIIMS, etc., must raise their own expectations. They must create their own internal pressure as the people around them do not expect them to go for targets that are considered big, and neither do they want that!

Dear aspirant, think along these lines. Why would a person from a college – that which is not among the top league colleges – want one of his friends to even set up the goal of civil services? For the demotivating person surely knows 2 things: a) that he/she does not have the will to sit back and study patiently for one year, and b) he/she may suffer inferiority if you crack civil services and that person is left behind in their career. Thus, he/she will use all the soft skills to terrorize you about UPSC Civil services preparations.

Thus, once you have made up your mind to sit for study, the best way to create internal pressure is to make your position public. Do not shy away or try to hide the fact that you are studying for UPSC. I have seen this tendency in many people. They study for civil services but never admit it. It reflects the insecurity of failure and makes you weak. This is not a trait of an administrator. You have to be firm on your decision, stick to it, and even face consequences if they arise. Be firm and polite to whoever asks you, "Yes, I am studying for civil services, and I expect your cooperation to the desired end." Try this. You will definitely find yourself stronger, and a group of such people will automatically reinforce each other, and those who are cynical about you will find some other victim!

D) What if all the attempts are exhausted, and I don't get through?

What would have been the fun in life if the future could be so deterministic? In every field, we talk of chances, and this study is no exception to this rule. The risk of defeat in this game is real, but it can be and has to be minimized. Make yourself a little more secure professionally. Taste partial success before the grand one. Fill in the forms of exams that are closely related to civil services, such as common graduate level SSC, Assistant Commandant, APFC, etc. Be vigilant of the new openings that are being created by the government.

Selection in any exam will help you in 2 ways for civil services: a) there will always be security in your subconscious mind that you have something to fall back on, and b) it will help you in the interview. *(Read in detail in the chapter on preparation for the interview)*

When I was filling in the form of junior engineer recruited by SSC, one of my college friends told me, "IITians are not supposed to do middle-grade jobs. It is pathetic that you are doing this." Never did he realize that I considered both SSC and engineering services to be stepping stones to the final goal. The same holds true when graduates from SRCC, College of Business Studies, or, let us say, NLUs are found filling the forms of common graduate-level examinations conducted by SSC. The argument that a particular exam is not up to my standards does not hold any water in it. Fill in for all those exams where you fit in, clear it, and be a little more secure.

E) If I don't get through CSE, even then I will surely make it into some state public service examination.

That is a myth. Do not fall prey to it. I would consider state public service examinations tougher than CSE simply for 2 reasons: a) the content and structure of the course are quite different from that of CSE, and there are differences from state to state as well, and b) the age limit is generally 5 years higher than that of CSE. This makes the competition tough as more mature and experienced minds are writing the exam.

The line of thought must be that the state PSC exams are not a cakewalk for those who are through with their CSE course and thus do not take solace in the above misconception and become complacent in their studies. You have to study with an altogether different approach for state PSC.

F) I have more attempts as I am from a reserved category. I will surely make it through in any one of these.

The most dangerous misconception. Can anyone quantitatively express what reduction in effort is allowable for a category student owing to his/her reservation as compared to the input of a general category student? If 6 hours of average daily study for one year is sufficient for a general category student to clear civil services, then 5 hrs may be sufficient for an OBC candidate, 4 hours for an SC candidate, and 3 hours for one who is an ST. It may be a laughable proposition for many if we try to quantify the efforts in terms of the number of hours of study for students in different categories.

One of my dearest friends belongs to a reserved category. He resigned from a prestigious private sector company in 2008 to study civil services. In 2009, I met him before the preliminary of CSE, and he said, "Don't you worry. I shall be an IPS one day. My attempts are many, and I know I will get through any one of these." In 2014, that golden attempt was yet to arrive!

Every candidate, irrespective of category, should study the maximum that is possible and write the exam to the best of his/her efforts. Has anyone from the category thought that we should write one question less in the exam because we have a category? Then why do we seek solace in the number of attempts? Dear aspirants from the reserved section, you must not take refuge in the thought that you possess a greater number of attempts than that of the general candidates. An aspirant should always consider the upcoming attempt as his/her last attempt!

G) I am from a Hindi medium and very much disappointed to see the result of CSE as far as Hindi students are concerned. What should I do?

I share the disappointment and concern for Hindi students, as many of us do. Thus, the peaceful protest in Delhi has found a voice among many circles of the government also. The root cause of their problem was CSAT. After speaking to some Hindi aspirants and taking into view the experiences of faculties who teach in Hindi, I came to the following proposition;

The contention of the Hindi medium aspirants is that the verbatim translation of comprehensions in English to Hindi leads to distortions in the meaning of paragraphs if read in Hindi and thereby in the questions of comprehension. Further, it is written that in case of any discrepancy, the meaning of comprehension in English will be upheld. Thus, the Hindi students reading the 'distorted versions' of the comprehensions have to refer back and forth to both versions of the same passage so as to draw concrete inferences. This not only decreases the accuracy of their answers but also consumes their precious time. Hence, the results of Hindi students in the first stage were dismal.

However, paper II of the preliminary exam qualifying solves the problem of the supposed disadvantage of the Hindi medium students. If the Hindi aspirant may feel that his/her English is not up to par, then you can refer to the section that deals with the preparation of the preliminary exam. The controversy has been further elaborated therein.

H) I have brainstormed very hard but have not yet discovered my reason for studying civil services. Should I start my preparation without knowing the exact cause?

As we have discussed, the transformation of personal reasons into broader social goals of civil services is an evolutionary process. The same applies to the profound introspection of these reasons. Therefore, it is no wonder that when you purchase your books, you may not know why you are doing so. You may enroll in some coaching by paying a hefty amount and still not be aware of a convincing reason for doing so. You may have invested in good accommodation in Delhi but are not sure whether it would produce fruitful results or not. These doubts and confusions will slowly melt away. In the meantime, remain patient but constantly pose questions to your mind regarding all these efforts. It may take you a full month of preparation to realize what your actual agenda for preparation may be. Thus, do not pause your preparation even if you have yet to decipher the cause.

I) My friends have joined the coaching team right from the time they entered their first year of college. Will it create an early start advantage for these aspirants when they appear for CSE after graduation?

Not necessarily. In fact, if the candidates are not serious enough, it would further diminish their chances of selection. Because the non-serious ones would have imbibed perverted and wrong concepts in the coaching, and it would be difficult for them to unlearn it when they begin their serious preparations. This scenario is analogous to the early head start given to IIT JEE aspirants by training students from class 8th. Does it increase their chances of selection? I don't think so. Further, the study environment of the coaching institute, which takes massive admission of college-going students, becomes more or less like a college classroom, the majority of which are the non-serious, non-compliant ones. Quality learning in such an environment becomes difficult for a serious aspirant. Thus, I would recommend that for a serious aspirant undergoing graduation, the best would be to concentrate on the area of his/her majors and, side by side, develop hobbies and interests as well as read classic novels of various genres.

J) If it is not intelligence, then what does it take to be successful at CSE?

Being intelligent is advantageous but certainly not the sole prerequisite to cracking CSE. When I refer to intelligence, I mean 2 things: 'academic intelligence' – that is, you must have a history of constant good grades whether in school or college and second, I refer to the high IQ scores in various standard IQ tests. Both are helpful but not sufficient conditions to crack CSE. Then what else is required? A reasonable man would put every good virtue in this domain – hard work, perseverance, concentration, focus, communication skills, memory, time management, etc. Haven't we heard it several times, and that too not from a single person or limited to a single exam? All these attributes are necessary; some are more essential than others, but without a smart strategy, all such efforts will be futile. This is the single most important goal of this book – to help you arrive at your own smart strategy for CSE by optimizing the usage of the limited energies which a person has at a given period of time.

PART – II

Civil Services – A Brief Glimpse of Exam

This chapter details the structural aspects of the Civil Services recruitment process, such as eligibility criteria for the exam relevant to different categories of students, the number of attempts available to them, including relaxations, the different services to which one becomes eligible for recruitment, and finally, the examination structure and weightage to each stage thereof.

An analysis of the above aspects is important from the perspective of career planning, as the aspirants are at a crucial juncture of their careers, and knowledge of these aspects can help them plan better and, consequently, mitigate the danger of unknowns in the process. Furthermore, the approach here is tactical or utilitarian and not historical, implying that the glimpse of the exam is not a commentary on its evolution (for which we would have to turn back pages to the beginnings in the Pitts India Act, 1784, and the Charter Act of 1793 when methods of recruitment were outlined). Only the present examination scenario and judgments related to any disputes regarding it are discussed.

❖ **Services covered by the Civil Services Examinations, 2018 (as per 69th Annual Report of UPSC):**

i) Indian Administrative Service.

ii) Indian Foreign Service.

iii) Indian Police Service.

iv) Indian P&T Accounts & Finance Service, Group 'A.'

v) Indian Audit and Accounts Service, Group 'A.'

vi) Indian Revenue Service (Customs and Central Excise), Group 'A.'

vii) Indian Defense Accounts Service, Group 'A.'

viii) Indian Revenue Service (I.T.), Group 'A.'

ix) Indian Ordnance Factories Service Group 'A' (Assistant Works Manager, Administration).

x) Indian Postal Service, Group 'A.'

xi) Indian Civil Accounts Service, Group A.

xii) Indian Railway Traffic Service, Group A.

xiii) Indian Railway Accounts Service, Group A.

xiv) Indian Railway Personnel Service, Group A.

xv) Post of Assistant Security Commissioner in Railway Protection Force, Group 'A.'

xvi) Indian Defense Estates Service, Group 'A.'

xvii) Indian Information Service (Junior Grade), Group 'A.'

xviii) Indian Trade Service, Group 'A.'

xix) Indian Corporate Law Service, Group A.

xx) Armed Forces Headquarters Civil Service, Group B (Section Officer's Grade).

xxi) Delhi, Andaman & Nicobar Islands, Lakshadweep, Daman & Diu, and Dadra & Nagar Haveli Civil Service, Group B.

xxii) Delhi, Andaman & Nicobar Islands, Lakshadweep, Daman & Diu, and Dadra & Nagar Haveli Police Service, Group B.

xxiii) Pondicherry Civil Service, Group B.

xxiv) Pondicherry Police Service, Group B.

❖ **The scheme of examination:**

The CSE is conducted in 3 stages – preliminary exam, mains exam, and personality test (interview). The preliminary examination is objective and qualifying in nature; that is, the preliminary score is not taken into consideration when calculating the overall merit of candidates. The main (subjective examination) score and the personality test score are added together to arrive at the final merit rankings.

❖ **The competitive toughness of examinations:**

As per the **69ᵗʰ Annual Report of USPC**, the following are the statistics on the Civil Services Examination 2018. The selection rate is calculated by considering the successful candidates vis-a-vis the total number of candidates who actually appeared on the exam/test.

Examination	Applications submitted	Candidates appeared	Successful candidates	Selection Rate	Selection Rate as a Percentage of Prelim Candidates
CS (Preliminary), 2018	10,65,552	5,00,484	10419	2.08%	2.08%
CS (Mains), 2018	10419	10246	1992	19.44%	0.40%
Personality Test for CS, 2018	-	1992	759	38.10%	0.15%

Thus, only 150 students were selected for every 100,000 students who appeared in the Civil Services (Preliminary) Examination in 2018, making it one of the toughest exams not just in India but in the world.

❖ **The plan of examination:**

The present structure consists of 4 stages of examination;

1. **Preliminary examination** – The examination consists of objective multiple-choice questions. This stage of the Civil Service Examination process is of a qualifying nature; that is, the marks attained in this exam are not added to the final score when deciding the rank and allocating the service. Yet, it is of utmost importance as this is the first stage of the examination process, and one needs to qualify for this stage to be eligible for the Civil Services (Mains) Examination. Moreover, due to the constantly changing nature of the exam and a high rejection percentage of ~98%, prelims become the most important stage, and one cannot ignore it at her peril. The prelims consist of 2 papers, namely, paper 1 of general studies (GS) and paper 2 of general intelligence/aptitude. Both papers are worth 200 marks each. The GS paper consists of history, polity, economics, geography, ecology, science and technology, environment, and current affairs, while the general aptitude paper that is paper 2, tests students on inferences of passages, mathematics up to class 10th level, decision-making questions (which may or may not be there), data interpretation questions, and any other time-tested dimensions of general intelligence and aptitude. However, only the Paper 1 score decides the merit of the candidates, and Paper 2 is a qualifying paper with set criteria of a minimum of 33 percent marks.

2. **Mains examination** – This is the second stage of the examination process and follows a subjective pattern. There are a total of 9 subjective papers, out of which 7 are considered for merit, while 2 language papers are of a qualifying nature. The 7 papers that decide a candidate's selection for the Interview stage are as follows:

Subject	Paper	Maximum marks	Weightage
Essay	Essay	250	14.29%
General Studies	GS 1	250	57.14%
	GS 2	250	
	GS 3	250	
	GS 4	250	
Optional subject	Paper 1	250	28.57%
	Paper 2	250	
Total marks		1750	

Thus, General Studies accounts for more than half of the marks and has become very important from the examination perspective. In fact, it may be argued that the effective weightage of General Studies is 71.43% since there is a high correlation between the syllabus of the GS papers and the Essay. The latter just tries to capture the analytical skills of the student in a more thorough manner, while the content of the essay would inevitably have to be borrowed heavily from the knowledge of the syllabus of general studies. In terms of the reward-to-effort ratio, the optional subject still tops the list and is, hence, very important. Paper 1 is the theory of the optional, while Paper 2 focuses on applications of theoretical premises. Thus, the choice of the right optional becomes an important decision with huge ramifications on the final result. What all optional subjects are available, why only 4 or 5 options sell like hotcakes, what is the game of normalization in the score of optional subjects, and how to scientifically choose an optional subject that aligns with your area of interest and graduation is discussed in the next chapter *"Deciding the Optional Subject."*

The marks required for clearing the Mains examination are decided by the UPSC based on its wisdom and discretion. The UPSC may also fix the minimum qualifying marks individually for papers that are considered for deciding merit. Based on the statistics made public by the UPSC, the mean score of the top 100 rankers in CS (Mains), 2018 was 863/1750 (49%), while for those below rank 100, it was 797/1750 (45%).

One should not forget the 2 qualifying language papers of the mains examination – the compulsory Paper B of English language and Paper A, for which the candidate has to opt for a language from the list of languages listed in the 8th schedule of the constitution of India. It is to be noted *that paper A on one of the Indian languages has been non-compulsory for the candidates hailing from the states of Arunachal Pradesh, Manipur, Meghalaya, Mizoram, Nagaland, and Sikkim (CSE notifications 2015-2019).* The minimum qualifying marks in both papers A and B are, at present, 25% of the total maximum marks, and papers A & and B are of matriculation or equivalent standard. Now, there is a big catch here. There have been aspirants confident of securing a call for the interview stage based on their own estimation of performance in the Mains examination but failed to qualify for the language papers. Hence, one needs to be cautious about the qualifying language papers and avoid the pitfalls of taking them for granted. What is even more disastrous is that once a candidate fails in compulsory language papers, his/her score in any other paper will not be revealed because they are not even checked. Thus, it leaves a candidate devoid of a quantifiable assessment of his/her performance in the main examination. Therefore, smartly tackling the compulsory papers without affecting your performance in evaluative papers of the main examination is of utmost importance, and this has been dealt with in detail in the chapter on *"Preparations for Mains examination."*

3. **Personality test** – The candidates who qualify for the Mains examination are selected for the final stage of the examination, i.e. the Interview or Personality Test, which is conducted at

Dholpur House in Delhi (the UPSC Headquarters, situated right next to the India Gate). The maximum mark on the personality test is 275, making the total marks of CSE equal to 2025. However, there are no minimum qualifying marks for the Interview. What qualities or attributes does the board judge in a candidate during an interview? The notification of CSE 2019 states that the candidate would be asked questions of general interest, and the intent is to judge the mental caliber of the candidate; that it is not just a test of their intellectual capabilities but also social traits, interest in current affairs, their mental alertness, critical powers of assimilation, clear and logical exposition, balance of judgment, variety and depth of interest, ability for social cohesion and leadership, intellectual and moral integrity. These qualities are judged not by interrogative cross-examination but by engaging a candidate in a dialectical method of conversation, wherein the mature minds of the board elicit relevant information (or the lack of it) from a candidate and hence form an opinion about the candidate.

It is evident that the interview stage is the most subjective assessment stage of the Civil Services Examination process as the personality factors viz the stereotypes, biases, value system, attitudes, and interests of not just the candidate are given a stage for performance but also of the interview Panel. These personality factors of the interview panel impact the interpretation and judgments arrived at. Then there is the demon of anxiety, which can very well bring out a very different personality of the candidate in front of the panel. The interview process, however, prone to such subjective and unpredictable elements, has been a subject matter of in-depth study in Psychology & Organizational Behavior for decades, and the UPSC, one of the most reputed institutions of the Indian administrative apparatus, is expected to live up to the best of standards ensuring that such biases are kept at bay and the most accurate judgment is made. All these factors have been discussed and deliberated upon in the chapter *"Preparations for the Personality Test."*

4. **Medical examination** – Here, the medical and physical fitness of the candidate is ascertained, and it is rare that a candidate is deemed unfit for all the services. For the purpose of medical examination, the civil services have been categorized into Technical and Non-Technical services. Technical services, like IPS, require a certain minimum standard of physical fitness, and a candidate may find himself eligible for non-technical services like IAS but ineligible for IPS. At present, there are 5 technical services that have more stringent criteria for parameters like vision, height, chest, chest expansion, etc. These technical services are:

Police Services, Group A.
Railway Traffic Services, Group A
Railway Protection Force, Group A
Delhi, Andaman, and Nicobar Police Services – Group B
Pondicherry Police Services, Group B

All other services are considered to be non-technical services for the purpose of medical examination. The exact medical requirements, appeal against the decision of the medical board, cautions to be taken before going for medical examinations, and medical examination for physically challenged candidates, etc., are dwelled upon in a later chapter.

❖ **Eligibility criteria for CSE:**

The eligibility criteria for UPSC CSE have always been one of the cornerstones of controversies and also get tampered with by political parties to gain some vote mileage. A good illustration in this regard was when an extra attempt was announced in 2015 for any candidate who had appeared in CSE 2011, who would have been otherwise ineligible under normal eligibility norms. Now, to understand eligibility norms, let us divide them into 4 aspects – nationality, age, number of attempts, and qualification.

1. **Nationality criteria;**

Service	Nationality criteria as per CSE 2019.
IAS, IPS & IFS	The candidate must be a citizen of India.
All other services	A candidate must be either: (a) a citizen of India, or (b) a subject of Nepal, or, (c) a subject of Bhutan, or, (d) a Tibetan refugee who came to India before 1st January 1962 with the intention of permanently settling in India or (e) a person of Indian origin who has migrated from Pakistan, Burma, Sri Lanka, and the East African countries of Kenya, Uganda, the United Republic of Tanzania, Zambia, Malawi, Zaire, Ethiopia, and Vietnam, with the intention of permanently settling in India. Provided that a candidate belonging to categories (b), (c), (d), and (e) shall be a person in whose favor a certificate of eligibility has been issued by the Government of India. A candidate whose case requires a certificate of eligibility may be admitted to the examination, but the offer of appointment may be given only after the necessary eligibility certificate has been issued to him/her by the Government of India.

Our civil services are open to certain specific countries, apart from Indian citizens.

2. **Age criteria;**

The candidate must have attained the minimum age of 21 years on the 1st of August of the year of the prelims examination. For example, for the CS (Prelims) 2019, if the candidate's date of birth was August 02, 1998, then he was not eligible to appear in the exam. The maximum age is again determined as of August 01 of the year of examination and varies according to the category of the applicant, as given below:

Category of aspirant	Maximum age	Age relaxation
General	32	0
OBC	35	3
SC/ST	37	5
Candidate ordinarily domiciled in the State of J&K during 1 January 1980 to 31 December 1989.	37	5
Defense service personnel disabled in operations during hostilities with any foreign country or in a disturbed area and released as a consequence thereof;	35	3
Ex-servicemen, ECOs, and SSCOs who have rendered at least 5 years of military service (as of August 01 of the year of CS (Prelims)) and then released (conditions of release to be seen from notification).	37	5
(a) blindness and low vision; (b) deaf and hard of hearing; (c) locomotor disability, including cerebral palsy, leprosy cured, dwarfism, acid attack victims, and muscular dystrophy; (d) autism, intellectual disability, specific learning disability, and mental illness; and (e) multiple disabilities from among persons under clauses (a) to (d), including deaf-blindness.	42	10

OBC/SC/ST candidates who also qualify for other criteria will be eligible for cumulative age relaxation. For example, an OBC candidate born in 1988 in the state of J&K shall have a cumulative benefit of age relaxation equal to 3 + 5 years = 8 years; that is, the maximum age will be 40 years for that person.

The age is calculated as of August 01 of the year of the CS (Prelims) examination. Age-proof for the commission is $10^{th}/12^{th}$ or university/graduation certificates. Strangely, it doesn't accept extracts from the birth records of municipal corporations as age-proof! And, of course, Horoscopes are also not accepted as valid proof of age.

3. **Number of attempts:** These vary as per the category of the candidate and are as follows:

Category	Maximum number of attempts.
General	6
PH general	9
OBC	9
SC/ST	No limitation

PH general and PH OBC have the same number of attempts, everything else being the same. It is observed that many candidates give the prime of their youth and occupational career to the Civil Services Examination, and as luck would have it, many still are unable to land their dream job. It is of paramount importance that one realizes that Civil Services is just one of the career choices to excel in life, and the candidate should be honest in his own assessment of self to make a call when it is time to exit and not fall into the trap of escalation of commitment. The best-mitigating strategy is to continue pursuing a parallel stream in the occupational career, either in the form of higher education or some other job, which allows the candidate to manage the civil services exam along with other commitments. Ideally, the candidate may completely dedicate one to 2 years to the exam, and if not successful, then should pursue the above-mentioned strategy as after that, it is mainly revision and answer writing, which is enough to sharpen the blunt edges. Otherwise, the anxiety can take hold of an aspirant's mind and lead to depression. It is of paramount importance that beyond a self-determined time frame, as per one's background, the candidate feels his career is progressing exclusively in civil services. Further, the above guidance gains merit in the context of the fact that the number of attempts has changed in the past, and one should not put all eggs in one basket in case of attempts cut in the future.

4. **Qualification** – The candidate must hold a graduation degree or its equivalent from any university of center or state or deemed university or recognized college by UGC. Thus, parents should be very careful when selecting a private college for admission to their wards, as the degree from some of these may be in dispute under the judiciary. However, the aspirants who are in the final year of their graduation and are yet to be awarded the degree can definitely sit for the preliminary examination. But for the main examination, be assured that a degree is required. When you apply for the main examination, you are required to submit the graduation degree. Here, even the provisional degree will suffice, and the original can be produced at the time of the interview.

In some cases where medical students are concerned, doing an internship has now become a part of the compulsory curriculum, without which an MBBS degree may not be awarded. UPSC, in this regard, gives leverage to the extent that the internship certificate may be produced at the time of the interview or a certificate from the concerned authority from the college that the candidate has completed all the requirements (including internship, if any) for the award of the degree.

These are the basic eligibility requirements for CSE conducted by UPSC. One more peculiar one is that an aspirant should not be an IAS or IFS to take the exam again. He/she should first resign from the job at hand and then write the exam. This is done to discourage aspirants selected for IAS/IFS from writing the exam again. Everyone knows that there are some favorite cadres and others which are not preferred states in IAS. Similarly, some countries are more preferred and considered "hot spots" of working/deputation in IFS. These are allotted based on All India ranks and vacancies that are available. People who are allotted the so-called less preferred countries in IFS and 'difficult' states in IAS always have an incentive to write the exam again and upgrade their rank. However, we, as a country, need people to be posted in these tough domains, whether in India or outside. Thus, UPSC has rightly made a tougher criterion for IAS/IFS to write the exam again. One has to take a huge risk of quitting the existing service and slogging again for UPSC.

In this regard, let me share an example of a friend who got selected for IAS in 2014 and, in his category, was a later rank holder. He was allocated one of the so-called tough cadres of north-eastern India. Evidently, that friend vented out his frustration in the following words, *"For the first time in my entire life, I felt that this category of mine doomed me. Had I been in the general category, I would have landed in your service and spent the rest of my life in a peaceful manner. But unfortunately, I am doomed in that tough terrain as I don't carry any energy to write this exam again, and I have no other equivalent job in the corporate sector."*

Thus, my dear friends, this risk of being allocated hard areas and tough countries is pretty real. But someone has got to do it, hasn't it? This must not demotivate you as the government provides enough opportunities for deputation later on, along with preferred posting criteria after one hard posting of a specific tenure. Life is indeed much bigger, and it should not be painted in a single pale color by this so-called tough scenario!

Deciding the Optional Subject

It is imminent that UPSC is trying to reduce the weightage of the optional subject in CSE. In 2013, 2 papers of the optional subject were replaced by those of General Studies. Before that, there were 2 optional subjects to be selected for the mains examination, and these 2 options were of such importance that one could get through civil services by scoring 300 plus marks in both optional papers, even if GS scores were below average.

However, it is worth noting that even in the present scenario, the optional papers determine selection and influence the rank to a large extent. We must acknowledge the fact that it is difficult to create a significant lead in GS. After a rigorous one-year study, the serious competitors have more or less the same quantum of knowledge in GS. Some may have economics as a stronghold; others may fare better in History and Geography. Therefore, at the end of the exam, we realize that the range of marks of GS out of 1000 is not much. Here, the marks of the optional subject become the rank booster. The target score in the optional subject should be 250 out of 500 for both papers, that is 50%. Anything above that is your bonus!

With the kind of importance the optional subject carries, it is imperative that one should do a lot of brainstorming before choosing any optional subject. If you revert back to your decision, that is, you change the optional subject at any time, the time of study increases by at least 5 to 6 months. I have seen people changing their optional paper on the third attempt after 2 unsuccessful attempts and then managing to get into the list. But why be baffled and tormented by the wrong decision of the optional and waste even a single attempt? It is better to brainstorm for 2 months to decide which option will go with the aspirant rather than make a quick decision and waste an attempt or 2 before reversing the earlier decision. For this, a broad understanding of the guidelines is required to decide the best optional subject. The final decision must rest with the aspirant, but that decision must be an informed one incorporating the following facts and factors;

1. Optional subjects must be looked upon as static or dynamic subjects:

Static subjects have a well-defined syllabus that remains unchanged at the graduate level. For example, history and philosophy in art subjects, physics, chemistry, and mathematics in science subjects, and all engineering subjects; accountancy for commerce students; zoology and botany for medical students – these all can be categorized as static subjects. The content of these subjects remains the same in any year. Variations can be made in the questions, and that too in words, figures, and inferences. The essence remains the same.

On the other hand, dynamic subjects are evolving subjects in both essence and content, such as public administration, sociology, management, and law. The questions from these subjects will take into account recent developments, trends, phenomena, and case studies. You have to constantly update your knowledge regarding these subjects. Then, there may be some intermediate subjects, such as geography and psychology, which involve both static and dynamic concepts in almost equal proportions.

But the question is, which one should you go for? Dear aspirant, you must be fully sovereign to decide for yourself so that you can hold yourself accountable and no one else for the result of your examination. Do not be swayed by your peer circle. It does not mean that you should not hear others' opinions. You must have a full understanding of the experiences of others regarding an optional subject. Talk to those teachers and faculties who deal with general studies and extract their valuable views regarding the optional subjects. Nevertheless, don't go to subject experts asking for which option to choose. Why would a physics teacher advise you to go for public administration and vice versa?

Some may find a static subject more favorable as continuous deliberations on the subject are not required – once you study history, you only have to revise it and not incorporate new knowledge or inferences with changing times. However, there is another school of thought that finds dynamic subjects interesting and possesses a keen eye to relate to current issues and unfolding events in their optional subject, such as the one we find in public administration.

As far as my experience is concerned, I had no propensity for evolving dynamic subjects. I believe in one-time effort, even if more than average is required, and then reaping benefits for a longer period of time. Moreover, I was reluctant to take up arts subjects as I felt already burdened with the general studies portion. Thus, the choice for me was limited and quite apparent, that is, civil engineering – the subject of my graduation. This would also serve as my instrument to become professionally secure by competing and clearing the engineering services examination.

However, the aspirant must know that I was met with severe resistance when I mooted the idea of taking up civil engineering as an option in civil services. The general perception is that people do not make it into civil services while opting for engineering subjects as their optional subjects. This is true because a small proportion of aspirants go for engineering subjects. Thus, it is no surprise that when the notification for CSE 2013 quashed one optional subject, my mind was pulled in 2 different directions, with philosophy and civil engineering competing with each other for the one optional subject that I had to fill in. Finally, I decided to cling to civil engineering, taking into account the various repercussions and advantages of my decision, and it paid hefty returns when I secured exactly 250 marks in the optional.

2. Subjective and objective optional subjects:

Where the answers are not subject to different interpretations, the subject may be called objective in its essence, such as engineering subjects, science subjects, accountancy, etc. On the other hand, some involve subjective interpretations, such as art subjects. Objective subjects are generally static, while subjective subjects may be static or dynamic in their essence.

In contemporary times, where unpredictability in results has increased due to subjectivity involved in CSE owing to the increased weightage of GS, it is better if one goes for an objective optional subject. However, these are limited in scope. For example, a mechanical optional would be taken by only a mechanical engineer and not by any other engineer or art student. Thus, subjective subjects of a static nature should be the most preferable option for those aspirants who cannot opt for an objective optional subject, such as history, philosophy, anthropology, etc.

3. The concept of normalization of marks in optional subjects:

The underlying concept of normalization of marks in different optional subjects is to eliminate or reduce the distortions in marks produced due to the different toughness levels of each distinct optional subject. How do we counter the variations of marks resulting from the different toughness of each paper? What will happen if most of the marks in geography are less compared to those in sociology? Will the aspirants from geography be unsuccessful if, for a particular year, the paper is very tough and most of the scores are low? The answer to all these questions is the normalization of marks in each optional subject across various subjects. I won't dwell on the mathematical details of normalization as UPSC never discloses the methodology on its website or elsewhere. However, those aspirants who are interested in the nitty-gritty of the matter may go to the website of IIM Bangalore, where the full process is disclosed and used in CAT every year.

The question to be addressed here is what we infer from the fact that normalization exists. The inferences are 2;

a) One cannot choose an option by saying that a particular option is easier because it has fewer syllabuses or that the questions are easy in that option. The easier paper of an option would attract higher scores, and these marks, when normalized, would be scaled downwards.

b) The second inference is of utmost importance. Whatever optional an aspirant may choose, he/she must get into the top 1 or 2 percent of the scores in that optional. This makes it redundant, the fact whether the paper is tough or easy. In the former case, normalization would inflate your scores (when the paper is tough), and in the latter, it will lead to downscaling. But in both cases, you shall be among the top scorers in that particular option, and your chances of making it to the final list would tremendously increase.

The Menace of the Coaching Industry

The coaching industry exploits the fear psychosis of the aspirants. The contention of the institutes is that they aid and assist in the preparation of an aspirant. Right from familiarizing with what civil services are, its basic tenets, the pattern of examination, and the recent changes, the coaching industry grills the aspirant via its classroom programs, test series, and mock interviews so that they become fit to join civil services in the eyes of UPSC.

It cannot be denied that coaching is more required for the less self-motivated candidates. It tends to create regularity in studies by the push factor of the speedily advancing course and the pull factor of the fellow batch mates. Every aspirant faces a paucity of time in this preparation where the course is enormous. Here, the concise notes and the study material given by the coaching institutes may also help the candidate if used wisely.

However, the other side to this story is far from being innocuous; in fact, dismal is the word that I should use. Most of the big names in this industry are playing with the dreams of the aspirants. They are using pure marketing techniques to attract students from every segment and from every corner of the country. And friends, these fraudulent techniques are not unknown to us. In 2012, I was in search of a coaching program suitable to my needs. I ventured to some big coaching institutes and found that each of them claimed at least 500 selections of their own among the total of 1100 or so! How? Each of these coaching institutes conducted mock interview sessions of successful candidates during the main examination. Most of the aspirants register to appear in the mock interviews at 2 or even 3 different coaching institutes. The result is the high overlapping of the names of successful candidates in various institutes.

When I became suspicious of these replicating results of coaching institutes, I tried to discern some other ways of selecting the one which was 'perfect' and which could sail me through this civil services preparation. I got hold of The Hindu newspaper and started reading it for a few days. On one fine day, I found an open invitation to attend a seminar by one *'success guru.'* That advertisement repeated itself continuously for 3 or 4 days. I finally registered myself for that miraculous seminar. During the seminar, the *'success guru'* gave us an insight into civil services and various benefits of his institute, and he also introduced some of the toppers of that year. Those selected candidates spoke so highly of the institute that I was impressed and decided to join that institute by submitting a fee of around Rs. 40,000/-.

After attending the coaching on weekends for 3 weeks, I could perceive the hollowness of the education that the institute was providing. The teachers were incompetent and least concerned about the welfare of students, and the learning mechanism was absolutely focused on rote learning. I was fortunate enough to have perceived the system and left it with the least damage done to my concepts and vision; otherwise, I would not have been selected to write this book. Only financial damage was done to my pocket after I was denied a refund by the 'glamorous' institute! There would have been numerous such aspirants who had shared the same fate and parted ways with their hard-earned money for the elaborate yet hollow coaching programs.

The nuisance is not limited to the replication of results only. It stretches in various dimensions from thereon, and the impact on the aspirants is significant if he/she is not aware of the full facts regarding these institutes. Look at the offerings of various coaching institutes. Some of these are vying for candidates just after schooling! They have started a three-year program for those aspirants who are in the first year of their graduation. It is my sincere advice to our younger generation that they must not fall prey to the greed of these institutes. The dividends reaped will be much higher if a college-going student focuses on his/her graduation courses rather than studying for civil services during the college days.

Another flaw in these study schedules is that they are deliberate. The industry has thrown an unchallenged assumption that the more teaching hours there are, the better it is for the student, and hence, the popularity of the institute increases! It seems to me that studying in a coaching center has become something like going to an office – the difference is that here you have to pay a hefty charge for occupying a seat in that 'office.' The classes run up to 6 or 8 hours for 6 days, or maybe 7 days in a week! And why should the big players not be delighted to give such programs to the aspirants? After all, they have to charge up to 1.5 lac from a student, so he/she must be engaged for a good period of time throughout the course. The corollary of this engagement is that the faculties taking such extended study courses are left with no other option but to provide very detailed descriptions of the subject matter, which, apart from being redundant, creates an unnecessary burden on the aspirant. Many, thus, quit during the coaching, and some even drop the idea of preparations.

I believe teaching to be a noble profession. However, my practical experience in the coaching industry, both as a physics faculty teaching students preparing for IIT JEE and as an aspirant for civil services, forces me to change my belief system. Yet, there are some people in this industry who see the profession not only as a profit-making venture but also as a social responsibility. Sankalp Academy is one among those few. The entire machinery of the institute, along with the prominent teachers associated with it, is working with a mission to deliver the best guidance to those aspirants who can't afford the expenses of preparations at market rates. My association with Samkalp was only for a short duration, specifically for an interview. During this period, I was very well-versed in the method of functioning of the institution. One peculiar aspect that struck me was the discipline of the aspirants, which is required to inculcate in them the character and ethos of civil servants. However, Samkalp is limited in its capacity, and such endeavors are few to serve such a large number of aspirants throughout the country. Another highly effective program is the essay in the main paper offered by the RIAS Academy. A small academy, with not so marvelous infrastructure, is able to deliver the best quality service at a very reasonable price. What is commendable is the approach of the teacher, Dr. B. Ramaswamy, whose solemn belief is to remain always approachable to the aspirant as opposed to that of a 'celebrity faculty' who would vanish after taking the class of 200 plus students! The institute's GS test series was highly exhaustive and consisted of more than 30 papers. These papers are to be written in a time-bound manner and in a fixed-space scenario. Proper evaluation of the answers by Dr. B. Ramaswamy and suggestions thereupon were appreciable. Yet, such academies are few, and I expect that they would expand their infrastructure. I also hope that certain other such initiatives will come to light.

With the role of the coaching industry far from being minuscule in the present scenario, there have to be considerable reforms in this particular segment dealing with civil services. Think about it, my dear friends and future aspirants. What you require are not elaborate, extensive, and exhaustive coaching programs but short guidance techniques and interactions at a personal level with the faculties. These interactions will serve a purpose once you have read the basic texts for the subject matter, which you will find explicitly written in the coming chapters on preliminary and mains. Such a demand from the market will force the coaching institutes to restructure their courses, making them more interactive rather than promoting rote learning. Consequently, the fee structure would then have to be relaxed to a considerable extent as the number of hours will reduce drastically. If, instead of full-fledged classroom programs, we find the acceptability of short and sweet guidance modules.

I don't know how and when this gross error of the institutes will be realized by the aspirants. The sooner it happens, the better it becomes. Nevertheless, at present, we must delve into divergent analyses of the myths and FAQs related to the coaching sector so as to arrive at some general loopholes and benefits of the same.

Role of Newspapers, Magazines and Websites

Newspapers play an undisputed role in disseminating information, enhancing the power to comprehend essays, articles, and passages, and simultaneously adding to your vocabulary. However, the difference between blind reading and smart reading has to be clearly understood. The former is reading every single item in the newspaper, while the latter is picking the items that would bear significance in your exam. Thus, reading newspapers is an art and has to be learned through practice.

Again, your interest must not dominate your goal. An aspirant may be interested in sports, but reading that section would not be considered important from the examination point of view. Therefore, I have broadly listed the topics which you should not read, and if you do so, please do not include the time spent on it as part of your study time;

1. The sports section can be entirely left out.

2. International news that doesn't involve India.

3. Political debates, comments of spokespersons, and heated arguments shall be left out completely.

4. A book review is not required at all.

5. Historical reviews of political events.

The news section, which you should read, comes with a rider attached;

1. Political news has to be dealt with separately. You have to focus on the political aspect of that news, which shall be learned in the section dealing with the main examination.

2. The state news should be read to the extent that involves only some new schemes or policies.

3. The finance/economy section must be watched for policies of the finance ministry, actions of the RBI, and upcoming legislation dealing with finance. No pain should be taken to remember the periodic reviews of GDP, interest rates, import/export, and other facts and figures.

4. Business section must be read to the extent of performance of a particular sector. Movement of stocks, speculations of currency, mergers, and acquisitions can be left.

5. Science and Technology can be left out if you read the consolidated developments in the monthly magazine *'Science Reporter.'*

The topics which you must read completely;

1. Look out for Supreme Court judgments.

2. The Editorial section.

Thus, we see that an aspirant has to read the newspaper smartly enough so that the maximum can be extracted from minimum effort.

Magazines will confuse you. There are so many different magazines available that an aspirant may be tempted to overload themselves with myriad contents upon visiting the bookstall. Furthermore, there are diverse views emanating from the teachers, peer groups, and even the bookstall people regarding which magazine to study.

In this pandemonium that exists, I adhered to a clear-cut choice, that is, Yojana and nothing else. Initially, I took off with Frontline and then switched to Pratiyogita Darpan. I also tried The Gist, which gives the conciseness of several newspapers and magazines. But finally, I stabilized at Yojana. The publisher is the Information and Broadcasting Ministry, but it does not voice government views only.

Dear aspirant, compare the main paper of 2013 with the content of Yojana of the previous 7–8 months, and you will be amazed to find many questions in paper 2 and paper 3 of GS can be traced to several articles in Yojana. The monthly magazine is also important in an essay as it is forward-looking, prospective, and optimistic in its approach. The multi-dimensional analysis of an issue, its multi-sectoral linkages, challenges thereupon, and finally – instead of a negative view – a goal-oriented solution with a vision for development is what is required not only in your essay but also as a personal trait to be an administrator. Yojana suffices in this regard completely.

Kurukshetra, a publication of the Ministry of Rural Development, is also considered equivalent to Yojana in its content and importance. However, I feel that it is more research-oriented and provides a detailed solution to a problem rather than a generalist view. Taking this factor into account, I would suggest the aspirant stick to Yojana and read it thoroughly.

Websites may become a trap if not used astutely. There are so many websites that give facts and analysis, including the traditional part of the GS course. Websites such as civilsbaba.co.in, Iasbaba.com, mrunal, and unacademy are good in this regard.

However, the aspirant has to be very cautious when using these sites. You should know precisely what you are looking for on the internet. Otherwise, the abundant material available on the internet will sway you from your target, and you will end up reading a lot but knowing nothing! The internet, if not used properly, is bound to create distractions. Once, I set out to search for the program REDD, a mechanism at the world level to incentivize tropical developing countries to preserve their forests. It took me 4 hours on the internet to learn the basic intent, funding mechanism, and how it is linked to joint forest groups in India. Some days later, I found the same content in a more structured manner in some coaching notes!

Thus, in the language of economics, the ICOR (incremental capital-output ratio), that is, the change in output upon increasing a unit input, is definitely higher for internet studies. Therefore, dear aspirant, it is advisable to resort to the internet only when it is urgent and exit immediately once your task is achieved.

General Traps, Myths and Frequently Asked Questions

1. I am from IIT. Thus, I must take physics, chemistry, and mathematics as optional subjects.

This is the most prevalent myth among the IITians, and why not should it be so? They have cleared the toughest entrance to the engineering field by playing with P/C/M. However, one must not extrapolate their knowledge without concrete facts. Whatever we have studied at the intermediate level in P/C/M amounts to only a minuscule fraction of the course of these science subjects at the graduate level for CSE. One must be aware of the fact that the physics of CSE as an optional subject is very unlike what we have studied at the intermediate level, which calls for the least use of memory – most of the formulas can be derived if you are conceptually sound. This phenomenon is missing in the optional subject of physics. You have to remember a lot, and in that, too, in diversified areas, empirical in nature, with a set pattern of solving questions.

However, it is not that one should not take a science subject – it is blessed with the static nature of the subject itself. Thus, a thorough study of the subject can work miracles for you. The point is that one should not take P/C/M as an option in CSE solely because he/she finds past performance in these subjects magnificent. The idea should be that a prior acquaintance with the subject, along with the fact that it requires one-time hard work because of its unchanging nature, will work in the exam.

Digging deeper, if a comparative analysis of P/C/M is asked, then I would prefer chemistry to physics and mathematics because of the simple reason that the course is a little more well-defined and less complex in chemistry than in the other 2. This is my personal feeling drawn from the experiences of my peers, consisting of their journey through the course, the practice required, and finally, the results that it yielded in various attempts. The aspirant may have his/her independent, different, but firm views regarding the same.

2. People do not choose engineering subjects as their optional.

This myth takes root because we do not see many people opting for engineering subjects as optional, and thus, we do not find many in the final list. This fear of engineering subjects is the result of 2 things. Firstly, those engineers who decide to sit for CSE are mostly average and below-average students with insufficient knowledge of the engineering subject taught in college. Secondly, the coaching industry has yet to market engineering subjects as a fruitful option in CSE.

Dear aspirants of engineering background, do not be afraid of engineering subjects despite performing poorly in your graduation. Though the subject will take more time to be thoroughly studied, the results will be productive. These subjects are objective in essence; that is, you will get close to one hundred percent marks if your answer is correct.

Thus, I request you that in this scenario, where the weightage of GS has increased leading to a high level of subjectivity in evaluation, it is better to take an optional which is objective in its essence. Engineering subjects are fit in this regard, in fact, better than the science subjects!

3. One should take an option that is interesting to study.

Not necessarily. It is another myth. Your solemn interest should be to clear CSE and nothing else. How can you decide before studying any subject, just by its name or its content, whether this option would be interesting enough to study? Further, studying always suffers from procrastination (the habit of wasting time on activities apart from studying). Thus, it is better to choose optional rationally than by what you perceive is your interest.

I will take my example. I had always been interested in psychology throughout my college days. Sigmund Freud fascinated me to the extent that I read his 7 books and made notes out of them rather than studying civil engineering, which I was supposed to do to become a BTech civil engineer from IIT Roorkee. However, even though I found psychology to be an interesting subject, I did not opt for it as my optional subject in CSE. My decision was based on pressing needs such as the urge to be secure professionally, reducing the subjectivity of assessment, and introducing a static study of one-time hard work.

Thus, my dear aspirant, let me assure you of the fact that no subject is interesting to study. The motivation to study will arise not from your interest in the subject but from your desire to achieve the goal.

4. Optional, which is a part of GS or related to it, should be taken. It will make your work easier.

This statement is partly correct. Look at the explicit listing of the GS syllabus. Try to decipher which optional subjects share their course with GS. History, geography, political science, economics, philosophy, sociology, public administration. The list will expand further. In the above list, some subjects are more closely represented in general studies, while others are represented to a minuscule extent. Thus, if we base our choice of optional only on the criterion that it should suffice our study for GS as far as that portion is concerned, then the clear choice is History and Geography, in that order of preference.

5. Some optional subjects have a section that is generalist in nature. Taking that optional will reduce the effort.

This is a risky myth. Subjects such as sociology, political science, and philosophy contain sections of paper that even engineering students may answer with knowledge of general studies. However, this argument doesn't absolve the aspirants from not studying those portions specifically. More insight and intellectual deliberations are expected of aspirants from these particular sections, which are general in nature.

In fact, in these sections, aspirants have to work a bit harder to create the difference between their answers and those written in a generalist approach.

6. Some subjects that contain a lesser course are easier to study.

Optional subjects have very different proportions of course content. Some are elaborate, such as the science and engineering subjects, and even some arts subjects like history, while others are concise in their course, such as philosophy and sociology. However, after understanding the concept of normalization, one must not decide on the optional subject based solely on this criterion. If the course of a particular option is shorter, more students will opt for it, increasing the competition. Thus, standing in the top 1 or 2 percent of students in that optional subject would become difficult. Therefore, the notion that subjects with less content require less study is entirely frivolous. Dear aspirant, if you choose such a subject, be prepared to revise it 2 or 3 times to achieve the perfection needed to rank among the top students in that optional subject.

7. Without coaching, you cannot clear CSE.

I haven't seen a single candidate, whether successful or unsuccessful, who has not been associated with a coaching institute in some manner or another. You may take the full package of GS, coaching for the optional, or go for subject-specific coaching; you may take only the test series or the interview guidance. In any case, you are associated with the coaching, and however minuscule, the contribution of a coaching institute does exist in your success or perhaps in your failure!

But the irony is that very few candidates clear CSE in the same year as that of the coaching. And why is this so? Because it is a challenge to balance the time between coaching and self-study. Coaching becomes treacherous the moment you attend only the coaching and study less in your room. It becomes your enemy when the maximum time of your entire day is consumed in the institute, and at night, you are too tired and fatigued to study alone in your room.

If you decide to join coaching, then enroll in the month of June/July/August so that the course may be completed by the month of March/April the following year, which will give you at least 2 or 3 months of self-study before the preliminary exam. If you have missed September, it is advisable that you study on your own. Read the preliminary and the main sections of this handbook, and you will find all the aid required for a starter to begin the studies from scratch.

Further, it is advisable that coaching should not be more than 3 hours a day and that too for not more than 3 or max. 4 days a week. Trust me, you need 2 or 3 days in a week to consolidate what you have studied in coaching. I must tell you the story of a girl who joined a very reputed coaching company targeting CSE 2014. I had written preliminary in 2013 when she had just joined the coaching. After a year, I got selected, and by that time, she had decided to quit her preparations. When I asked why, here is what she had to say, "Continuously for 3 months, I attended the coaching without any break, not even on Sundays, from 9 am to 5 pm. The course piled up, and registers of class notes had to be kept on a separate bed. I then realized that I can't target CSE 2014, and I may not even try for 2015 also!"

So, my dear friends, coaching should ease your preparation. A teacher must guide you as a philosopher and friend, and in the end, your decision to join coaching must help you come out with flying colors. Thus, one must be careful when choosing a program that suits your requirements rather than just going for the brand and crowd!

8. I am financially weak and want to join coaching, but I can't afford it.

There exists a huge difference in the fee structure of coaching institutes. Some may charge in lakhs, and others may charge around £40,000 for the same program. But you must understand that the fee is not a reflection of the quality, dedication, and commitment the faculty may offer to its students. It is evident that these coaching institutes have become unaffordable for the EWS of society. This is an area to work on. We are also evaluating the possibility of some guidance programs as opposed to the stereotyped spoon-feeding costly coaching classes for civil services. Evidently, there will be a huge difference in fees, which may give a breather to economically disadvantaged students.

9. Is subject-specific coaching better than studying for the whole GS?

Subject-specific coaching is undoubtedly better. It offers greater flexibility in terms of timing and content and is much better priced compared to the complete GS course. Also, there are good faculties offering their expertise in particular subjects. However, the faculties of these individual subjects must transform their teaching pattern from a unidirectional information flow system to interactive sessions advocating dialectical methods of learning. I have absolutely no hope from the big players in this industry that they may constitute batches of around 50 students or fewer and try to treat an aspirant in a more humane manner rather than just as 'another customer in our shop.'

10. Most coaching institutes are in Delhi, so I have to stay in Delhi during the coaching and until I get through CSE.

I don't perceive the logic of staying in Delhi after the coaching is over just for the purpose of studying. My known friends, who are mostly from outside Delhi, assert that there is no atmosphere to study at home. Maybe! But I personally find no better place to study than my home. I understand that it is difficult to get a cozy environment in which to study in a joint family, but the same can't be held true for a nuclear family. In fact, the home will offer you many other conveniences such as hygienic food, timely sleep as per the biological clock of the body, and emotional connection with immediate family, which may comfort and help you get over failures, if any.

Another argument I come across is that once you leave Delhi for your hometown, you will be lost in touch with what is happening in current affairs. "You must know what people are studying and what the latest study material of reputed coaching institutes in the market is." One of my close friends from Lucknow, who had been staying in Delhi for 4 years, told me when I asked him the reasons for his affinity to Delhi. However, I felt the reason was too naïve to hold water. You can have friends in Delhi who may update you on any new material of importance, or you may call the coaching institute directly or visit its website for new information.

Let me have the privilege to request, at least, those aspirants who belong to areas adjoining Delhi to return to their homes after the coaching is over and the preliminary examination is taken. You may enroll in some weekend test series and collect whatever material you may require for your main preparations.

11. Which is better – printed study material or the class notes? Or should I study the standard textbooks?

Indeed, the standard textbooks of NCERT and those referred to during graduation are the best. However, the material becomes so exhaustive and segregated that due to the paucity of time, it is difficult to read, filter, and assemble the required content separately. It is this need that the coaching institutes satisfy through their printed notes and the class notes.

Now, whether to study the standard text or the coaching material would depend on the timing of the question and the course that is required to be studied. For example, it is written that Indian culture is in the syllabus and not the Indian ancient or medieval history. But Indian culture, comprising art, architecture, literature, dance, drama, and music, developed during this time. So, an aspirant has to study the ancient and medieval history of India with a special focus on alienating and connecting the developments in Indian culture.

Thus, if someone asks in the month of June how to study Indian culture, I would recommend NCERT books of history from classes 6th to 8th. Yet, if the same question is asked in October, my blunt reply would be to study the notes of a coaching institute. The second question is: which notes – class notes or printed notes? This depends on the convenience of an aspirant. I personally feel that printed notes would be better – no handwriting issues and no variations due to the subjective interpretation of the writer.

12. Should I take the test series?

A full affirmative reply to that question from my side. You should have net practice before the final match and mock drills before fighting at the front. Test series are required for both prelims and mains. At the final stage, mock interview practice sessions – maybe 2 or 3 – are required.

But there is a catch. That is of an escapist tendency. Some aspirants do not join the test series as they believe that their preparations are not up to the mark, while others who join the test series leave it without completion. Dear aspirant, you must accept the fact that one may never feel that his/her preparation is optimum for cracking civil services. How can one tell what the level of preparation is without writing tests? Moreover, the course of CSE is endless, and to get a strong hold in each and every topic is not possible and not required also.

One of my friends, in his third attempt after the preliminary in 2013, refused my proposal to join the test series of mains examination in the following words: "I will not join any test series until I remember every article of our constitution, most of the cities of the globe, report of every recent committee, along with challenges in every sector of India, and also India's relation with every other member country of the UN."

I didn't know many things he said. But I joined the test series and wrote all my tests seriously in a time-bound manner. Dear aspirant, you improve with every test you write, provided you are doing justice to your writings and taking pains to analyze what went wrong during the test papers.

13. Is coaching required for the optional subject?

It depends on whether the optional is entirely new to you or if you have studied it during your graduation, and how seriously. An engineer would definitely require some assistance in history as an optional subject. A science student who has been diligent throughout their college days may not need any external help in that subject if taken as an optional for CSE. On the contrary, those who were backbenchers during their graduation days may need assistance in their own subjects if taken as an optional. Therefore, after deciding on the optional subject, an aspirant must assess their previous level of knowledge in it and then decide whether coaching is necessary or not.

14. What basic checks must be done if you decide to join a coaching?

In this era of transparency, when the political parties & candidates are also expected to disclose some basic information to the public, should not the coaching industry follow these basic mandatory disclosures? The educational background of the faculties must be disclosed by the coaching institutes. Go to the website of the institute and check for this. Many coaching centers stress more on listing the fee structure for various modules rather than highlighting the profiles of the teachers.

Another strange phenomenon is that the optional subject may be taught by people with no educational background in that particular optional. Any optional subject requires specialist knowledge, in-depth study, and good experience on the part of teachers. It is not a cakewalk that one fine day a person may take a pledge that from now on he/she shall teach an optional subject and start teaching it! Public administration and sociology have been majorly plundered by 'quack teachers.' Thus, an aspirant must not fall prey to such prevalent misconduct.

15. How can I use a newspaper to perform better in comprehensions of CSAT?

Apart from playing an efficient role in GS preparations, newspapers can also be effectively used to improve comprehension of CSAT. Do the following and adhere to it regularly: Take any one editorial article. Try to read it within 3 minutes and write down its essence in another 3 minutes. Dear aspirant, make this a habit for around one month before the preliminary exam and see continuous improvement in your CSAT scores by taking any test series. Even if you are a Hindi medium student and CSAT remains, despite all the protests, I request you to follow this strategy and fare better than the English medium students as far as comprehension is concerned. I followed this practice for around 20 days before prelims and achieved 180 out of 200 in the CSAT paper in 2013!

16. Should I make notes of the newspaper?

Once you have understood how to filter the required content of the newspaper and read it smartly, then you must progress to the second level, that is making organized notes. However, the notes should be segregated and readily available for future reference. Dear aspirant, dedicate small diaries for polity & constitution, Geography & environment, Social issues & schemes, Economic policies, and International relations. Whenever you read the newspaper, write down the respective news and their analysis in a very concise and lucid manner in these dedicated diaries. This will aid you not only in GS but also in your essay.

17. If I don't read the newspaper, I won't clear CSE.

It is, in fact, better not to read the newspaper if you read it blindly. Dear aspirant, if you have tried smart reading of the newspaper and still could not pursue it in an organized fashion, then it's better to devote the time you spend on the newspaper to other pursuits. You will definitely find a collection of all the important issues in the Yojana magazine.

18. India yearbook is a must-read.

It is one of the most prevalent misconceptions. On the contrary, it is not required at all. It is so copious that the bulk would itself create hindrance for the aspirant to complete it and may lead to a frustrating attempt in this pursuit. In fact, the plan document is the best substitute for India year book. And that too has to be read carefully, particularly for the mains examination.

19. We must jot down new words encountered while reading the newspaper, along with their meanings from the dictionary.

Neither possible nor required. Not possible because you may lose the continuity of this particular habit of finding new words and writing their meaning due to the scarcity of time witnessed during these preparations. You would do it for a few weeks, and then other concerns will debilitate this habit. Furthermore, while you focus on the meaning of a particular word, the article as a whole would be displaced from your mind, and you might have to read it again!

Not required because more than the meaning of a particular word, its usage and the sense of the sentence are valued.

20. I feel let down by people who readily use mobiles to study newspapers and search anything on the internet. They accumulate vast knowledge and have a considerable edge.

Dear aspirant, if you have encountered this feeling, then you must acknowledge that you are a victim of the digital divide just like me! Still, we must understand that easy access to information is not the sole criterion that will govern your chances of success. It is how the aspirant processes that information, whether it is organized or not, can it be recalled for usage at a later point in time or not, what is the time invested to procure that information; all these factors combined determine the chances of success in current affairs.

Also, increasing your general knowledge alone won't help you much. These only provide supplements to your analytical answers in the mains as purely factual questions are not asked in mains examination. For example, why should I be bothered about who gets caught in the match-fixing scandal of the cricket world? But I am definitely concerned about its impact on sports, its financial linkages to the underworld and extremist activities, which laws our government law-enforcing agencies use to curb it, and whether there are any loopholes in those laws.

Another example, I may not remember who got the Nobel Prize in chemistry, whether it was shared or not, but I must know how that research will help mankind, will that be available to India and how. Thus, my dear aspirants, get over this syndrome to memorize the facts and dig deeper into the concepts that provide the facts before us!

PART – III

Preparations for Preliminary Examination

I personally find preliminary examination competitively tougher than mains! Look at the statistics, and you shall know why. Only 14,000 students are selected roughly from around 5 lacs appearing in any year; that is, more than 97 percentile is needed. The competition has become fiercer since the introduction of CSAT.

Further, the cut-off increased every year due to pattern predictability from 2011 to 2013. However, CSE 2014 is a departure from this trend of increasing cut-off every year. *Because there had been a last-minute change in the marking scheme of GS paper 2 for CSE 2014, another change in CSE 2015 was more or less expected to stabilize the marking scheme.* Thus, in this highly competitive atmosphere, an aspirant, especially a fresher, is baffled as to how to go about his/her preliminary preparations.

◈ Comparative Analysis of paper II, CSAT – 2014 and CSAT 2015

SECTION	QUESTIONS in CSAT 2014	QUESTIONS in CSAT 2015
Comprehension (printed in both English and Hindi).	26	34
Mathematics	18	24
Logical reasoning	19	13
Data interpretation	6	5
Figure based	5	4
English comprehension (written only in English)	6	Discontinued

CSAT, 2014, again reinforced our belief in the unpredictability of UPSC question-setting trends! The major surprise was the deletion of the decision-making questions from Paper 2. Moreover, the GS paper had an extreme nature – questions were either far too easy or considerably tough. In CSAT 2015, paper 2 was qualifying only with a minimum requirement of 33% across every category. However, despite that, I had seen some aspirants not clearing preliminary because they fell short of the minimum required marks in paper 2. Such candidates and those who do not feel confident yet in CSAT paper 2 must read the section *"Smart strategy for CSAT Paper 2"* given below in this chapter.

◈ The Earlier Controversy

The CSAT paper-2 had been the source of all controversy surrounding the preliminary examination to civil services. It was contended that the paper promotes English-speaking students, urban Indian population, and engineering and management background students. On the same lines, it creates a bias against Hindi-speaking and regional language-speaking aspirants, rural India, and humanities students. The following were the independent general views of various aggrieved sections;

a) **Hindi medium aspirants:** the section of English comprehension (written only in English), which tests the understanding of the English language, is biased against Hindi-speaking students. Furthermore, the conversion of other comprehensions into Hindi is verbatim and done through translating software, which results in the meaning of the paragraph being distorted slightly. Thus, the Hindi student has to refer to the English version of the comprehension intermittently to grasp the exact meaning of the text. This leads to a waste of time.

b) **Regional Language student:** What will a graduate do if he/she speaks Oriya and lacks both English and Hindi skills? Is it mandatory that graduates speaking other than Hindi must have sufficient functional literacy in English to write the CSAT exam?

Or is it expected that every graduate college offers functional literacy in English? Does this also amount to a preference of Hindi belt areas over the rest of India? Many tough questions remain here.

c) **Rural Aspirants:** Does language bias, as contended by Hindi and regional language students, lead to urban-rural divide widening through Civil Services Examination? The basic assumption for rural bias to exist would be that English is mainly the language of urban India, especially the metropolitan centers.

d) **Humanities students:** the contention is that mathematics, which has around 17 percent weightage, is above the standard of 10th class. Also, it is asserted that logical reasoning and data interpretation, which amount to 30 percent weightage combined, are more managerial than administrative. It is further argued that engineering and management students have a clear-cut advantage over humanities aspirants and, simultaneously, the administrative skills required for services can't be judged by this pattern of examination.

◈ The Present Scheme of Marking

The protest took off from Mukherjee Nagar, Delhi after the announcement of the final result of CSE 2013 by UPSC, and within 3 months or so, it captured the imagination of the people's representatives sitting in the parliament of India. To pacify the outrage, the government hurriedly proposed the following changes to be done by the UPSC for CSE 2014;

A) The marks of English comprehension (compulsory, which has no translation in Hindi) won't be counted in the final merit.

B) The aspirants who took the exam in 2011, the year when CSAT was introduced for the first time, would be given an extra attempt in 2015.

The government has tried to alleviate the concerns of the Hindi students by the above proposals. However, UPSC, an autonomous constitutional body, was unrelenting in its pursuit until the eleventh hour. With the change of chairmanship, the above-written modifications were notified in the Gazette.

There are several issues related to this supposedly trivial issue of removing compulsory English questions. The first and foremost deal with the autonomy of the constitutional bodies themselves. If UPSC is pressurized to change the pattern or the marking scheme at the last hour by the government, its autonomy will be questioned. And then the question pertaining to the autonomy of other constitutional bodies, such as the election commission and the comptroller and auditor general, may be brought into public debate.

The second issue is that the fiduciary value of the institutions has been challenged. The intentions of the people running these institutions and their capabilities have been debated. Are not the members of UPSC, who have been entrusted with the responsibilities to recommend civil servants to DoPT, doing justice to their jobs and thus, to the nation? Do they not have the vision and the corresponding autonomy to change the structure of the examination as per the requirements of the current times? These questions not only torment an aspirant but are also of concern to every common man because the process of selection of civil servants affects the nation itself.

The above pacifying act of the govt. rendered the pattern of the preliminary unstable – what would be the purpose of English comprehensive questions when their marks are not taken into merit? Thus, it was evident that CSE 2015 would attract a major change, at least in the preliminary part of it. And this happened. In preliminary 2015, paper 2 became only a qualifying paper with a 33% fixed minimum criteria for every category. The paper 1 of 200 marks would be considered for merit. The grievances of the protesting aspirants were addressed in a long-term constructive manner by the CSE 2015 notification, which has been elaborated in the later part of this book.

◈ The Way Ahead

As we have discussed earlier, the success of a candidate is not entirely through his/her own efforts. There is a direct external contribution from parents, family, and peers, and there is an indirect contribution from the society at large, which has to be virtuously returned to the society by public service. Thus, the discussion entails that there are certain factors beyond the reach of an aspirant that will influence the chances of his/her selection. The efforts must be directed to maximize the positive factors and minimize the negative factors as far as selection is concerned. Coming to the case of the alleged disadvantaged lot comprising Hindi students, regional language students, rural, and humanities students, their efforts were directed toward scrapping the paper 2 of the preliminary exam. As per their contention, this would have given them a level playing field and thus enhance the chances of their selection. However, the present mechanism of testing a basic level of proficiency in paper 2 and considering paper 1 for merit is certainly not adverse to the above-mentioned section of students.

Dear aspirants, certain things are beyond our control. Thus, after a point, one cannot change the external factors, and even if that change may occur, it might take time to transcend into action. That stage is important to realize, as after this, the aspirant has to let go of external factors and work on factors that he or she may control directly, such as the subject knowledge, language command, analytical skills, etc. With this in mind, one should set the right strategy for further preparations during the present times of volatility in pattern and marking scheme.

So what is there for an aspirant in all this turmoil and confusion? Many aspirants halt studies when there emerged a speculation that the date of the preliminary exam would be postponed to the month of September in 2014. It is in these times that clever aspirants benefit. The best way is to stay away from tea stall discussions. Avoid such news in the media – both print and electronic. Dear friends, the only source of confirmed change is a notification on the UPSC website or in the Gazette of India. Until that is done, do not be cheerful or sorrowful, but be disinterested in such speculative affairs. This disinterest won't allow you to dissipate energy without purpose. You shall hear everything at those times which suit you, resist giving proclamations about the speculations, and thus, no imprint would be left on your mind which could have consumed precious energy.

I will give you an example. In October/November 2012, there was widespread speculation that UPSC might do away with one of the optional subjects and in place of that introduce 2 more papers of GS. At that time, I had taken philosophy as a second optional along with civil engineering. While wandering to tea stalls, I encountered various opinions of what UPSC is going to do. The people spoke with so much conviction as if they were members of the committee which was to finalize the changes! I heard them silently, their strategy of going ahead during this indecisive period, whether to stick to doing optional or switch over to GS for the moment.

Although I heard talks, I avoided giving any opinion. A friend forced me to utter something in this regard. I said, "There is no confusion. Two options exist for me until the previous pattern is replaced by the new one through a notification in the Gazette. Thus, I continue studying philosophy along with GS."

Nevertheless, the notification of CSE 2013 did drastically alter the pattern. One optional was replaced by GS. The western philosophy and Indian philosophy, which I had completed, were now redundant. The people advocating a change in the pattern taunted me for my wasted efforts. "You remember I told you. Didn't I? It is not useful to study for civil services till the notification is released," one of my friends teased me. But he had neglected the fact that I was studying GS along with philosophy. He had further ignored the fact that I had been in continuous touch with studies, and he had taken a break. Dear aspirant, you must know that it is better to maintain continuity of studies rather than taking long breaks in between.

Coming to CSE 2015, there was quite a speculation before the notification of the changes that may be done in the preliminary. But, the aspirants for 2015 must have continued with their GS preparations until the notification for 2015 was out. Bothering about paper 2 before the notification for CSE 2015 was an utter waste of energy, which one should have avoided. Now, when the notification of CSE 2015 is out, one can plan accordingly.

◈ Smart Strategy for CSAT Paper 2

The pattern of the preliminary examination for 2015 and years after remains the same (that is, paper 2 is now qualifying only). It is expected that for CSE 2025, the pattern and marking scheme shall remain the same. Now, what should be the approach of an aspirant? How should he/she place the timing of his/her preparations? How to strike a balance between GS and CSAT?

Hereby, I present to you a strategy that is bound to give results if followed with commitment;

Step 1: Aspirants of CSE 2025 must be free from any coaching engagements at least 2 months before the preliminary examination.

Step 2: Join the test series of that coaching which gives a paper closest to what is asked by CSE. Weekly tests are preferable. 3 or 4 are sufficient.

Step 3: Simultaneously write the summary of any one article from the newspaper each day for at least 30 days. Hindi medium students must also do the same, either in Hindi or English, as per their convenience. This will also be helpful in GS.

Step 4: Get the question papers of any 2 other coaching institutes at your home so that diverse questions may also be accommodated.

Step 5: Give 2 or 3 CSAT papers at your home, almost equally spaced throughout the last 2 months; that is, after an interval of 7 or 8 days.

Step 6: Tests must be taken in a strict time-bound manner and completed within 1 hour and 50 minutes at home.

The analysis of the question paper must be diagnostic first and then a curative study. The first paper of CSAT paper 2 should be given unprepared. See closely which the problem area is and attack that area only. For example, consider an aspirant who is not able to solve logical derivation questions and blood relation questions in a particular time-frame. Why should he/she do speed – distance questions, data interpretation, geometry, and probability? Why should he/she not focus on just the problematic area and do around 30 independent questions each of logical derivations and blood relations? In fact, that aspirant was me, and I did attack only my weaknesses instead of covering every aspect of CSAT. The result was up to my satisfaction.

In the present scenario, there is also a tendency to neglect paper 2 altogether as it has become qualifying only and doesn't count in the final merit. This has become a trap for some. Avoid taking this paper 2 for granted and devote time to solve at least 3 or 4 mocks after the problematic area has been identified.

◈ Comparative Analysis of paper I, CSAT – 2014, CSAT – 2015 & CSAT – 2024

SECTION	QUESTIONS in 2014	QUESTIONS in 2015	QUESTIONS in 2024
POLITY	11	13	18
History	5	13	9
Art and Culture	15	4	
Geography	14	15	20
Environment (pollution)	4	3	10
Environment (Ecology)	16	10	

Science and Technology.	15	9	8
Economics	11	21	15
Current affairs, schemes, and international relations	9	12	20

(I wonder why the translation of GS paper 1 from English to Hindi didn't suffer from the alleged infirmity which exists in the translation of GS paper 2. Maybe because there are no long comprehensions in paper 1 that need to be translated like that in paper 2!)

As per the above analysis, the following conclusions can be drawn;

1. The weightage of art and culture decreased drastically in 2024, so there is a good probability that it may be sufficiently increased in CSAT 2025.

2. Economics increased and almost doubled in 2015, but then averaged out in 2024. Thus, there is a possibility that in 2025, the number of economics questions may average around 15-16.

3. According to me, 55 – 60 were easy to moderately difficult questions. The total attempt should have been around 85 questions at least, and I expect the candidate to be 90% correct in these easy-to-moderate difficulty level questions; that is, let us say, 54 questions correct out of 60. Out of the rest 25 questions attempted (which I assume to be tough to very tough), a candidate should have 30% accuracy; that is, 8 more questions correct.

4. Thus, a total of 62 questions, correct and 23 questions wrong, would render a candidate with a score of around 116. Thus, in this paper, a score of 114 – 118 is achievable and a decent enough score.

◈ Subject-wise Analysis

Polity: It is one of the most predictable and scoring parts of GS paper 1. A starter must first cover the fundamental aspects of our polity by reading NCERT class IX and class X textbook called DEMOCRATIC POLITICS. It will establish a sense of some basic polity terms – ideals, constitution, election system, power sharing, etc. There are almost no articles that are encountered here. Thus, it is very interesting with some prominent examples. After this, an aspirant is required to be familiar with the parts, articles, and the schedules of the constitution of India. For this, instead of going for the coaching notes, an aspirant must read a standard text such as Laxmikant along with the bare act. A concise substitute of Laxmikant is a book titled 'our constitution' by Subhash Kashyap. The candidate must read either of the 2 but not both. Please note that D.D Basu is an exemplary commentary on the constitution of India. Nuances to that extent may not be required for UPSC.

Those who have already studied polity once need not go through the entire standard text repeatedly. They should focus only on their weak areas or areas of particular interest. For example, curiosity may arise for an aspirant if they read that the verdict of the Cauvery tribunal is challenged by Tamil Nadu despite the fact that tribunal judgments are exempt from the jurisdiction of higher judiciary as per Article 262 (Parliament, by law, has provided for this exemption). That curiosity arising from the current polity of the country must be satisfied instantly by referring to the relevant parts of the bare acts. Thus, after one complete reading of polity, it should become a habit. Later on, we shall discuss how to extract the political news from the country's politics.

<u>Modern History</u>: Modern India is easier and should be done first. The questions are such that a broad idea of the chronological events and their causes and consequences is sufficient. This can be done by reading NBT freedom struggle, a concise 'novel' like book for those who find history boring. Read it like a novel, anticipate what would happen next, and when you are through with it for the very first time, it would set you up for a little elaborate texts in history. After the NBT book, an aspirant is in a position of critical analysis of NCERT books of class VIII titled as OUR PAST – III (both part 1 and part 2). Because the factual details are not asked in greater depth in CSAT, old NCERTs of modern history are not recommended. The above analysis is sufficient for prelims with regards to modern Indian history. Those who invested a lot of time in modern history were disappointed to see the easy level of questions. However, their knowledge will create a difference in the mains examination. An aspirant is advised not to reduce the study of the basic text in modern history by witnessing the easy questions of this paper.

Art and Culture: High fluctuations in the number of questions asked from this topic have been witnessed. It is expected that the questions will increase in the year 2016. Furthermore, this topic has been a cause of worry for many due to the opaque nature of the content; that is, the aspirants are confused about what to study and what not. Also, the next question is from where to study. With the presence of so much diverse and in-depth material, it becomes all the more confusing for the aspirant to select the relevant parts as per the exam requirements. Thus, regarding this, another separate section has been introduced which deals with both the preliminary part and the GS 1 of the mains. Readers particularly interested in this section may skip directly to the chapter on preparations for mains.

Geography: The subject can be divided into physical, human, and economic geography. Physical geography deals with the phenomena of atmosphere, hydrosphere, and landforms, their causes, and associated processes. Thus, physical geography has to be studied at a global scale, and some phenomena shall be peculiar to India, such as monsoons. Therefore, the suggestion is that a standard text dealing with world-level phenomena must be complemented by a text that is specific to Indian settings. The book J.C. Leong deals wonderfully with atmospheric systems, ocean currents, landforms, and their causes, as well as the interaction of abiotic factors with the biotic factors to create different biomes all over the world. Each biome has some generalized characteristics of temperature, rainfall, flora, and fauna. A substitute for this book would be NCERT class XI publication titled 'Fundamentals of Physical Geography.' Read either Leong or the NCERT book. But do not read both as it would be a repetition of work and count as redundant effort.

After getting a broad view of the global phenomenon, we have to study the particular case of India. This is well elaborated in the class XI textbook of geography titled as 'India physical environment,' which deals with our mountains, rivers, climate, vegetation, and soil. As we see in the analysis of GS paper 1 above, map-based questions were increased. Two questions from the world map were also included. Out of the 9 questions based on maps, 4 could have been answered quite easily. The rest needed specific knowledge. The following maps (on the physical map of India) are required to be practiced thoroughly with the help of an atlas;

a) Mountain, b) Rivers, c) national parks, d) wildlife sanctuary, e) tiger reserves, f) soils, g) vegetation

(Check out the difference between national parks, wildlife sanctuaries, and tiger reserves.)

The next part is human and economic geography. As far as preliminary is concerned, only the Indian context is required. Out of the 2, economic is more important, so we shall focus on it more. This entails a thorough reading of NCERT class VIII textbook titled as 'Resources and Development' and also of class X book 'Contemporary India – II.' For preliminary, these 2 books would be sufficient for dealing with mineral, agriculture, water, forest, and wildlife resources of India, location of industries, and factors influencing the same.

Human geography deals with human resources, human capital, and its management, including capacity building. This part has some areas in common with economics as well. Thus, we shall restrict our reading of human geography as questions directly dealing with it are not asked; the questions may be coupled with economics or current policies.

Therefore, the aspirants are advised to go through NCERT class XII textbook titled 'India – people and economy.'

<u>Environment:</u> This is a tricky subject as it has a vast overlapping domain with geography; it entices aspirants to repeat their efforts leading to time wastage and no significant knowledge addition. However, we shall precisely focus on what composes our analysis of the environment. It can be broadly divided into ecology, biodiversity, and pollution. The standard text in ecology is NCERT class XII biology textbook where an aspirant is advised to read unit X titled as ecology. Look at the previous years' questions, and you shall find that many of the questions can be tackled using the fundamental knowledge in the above-mentioned text.

Biodiversity and pollution are orderly presented in the 'Teachers' handbook on Environmental education for the higher secondary stage' in the last 4 chapters. There is another standard text called 'Environmental studies for graduate' by Erach Bharucha. Both are thorough in their analysis. Thus, an aspirant is advised to read the teachers' handbook first and then the wildlife part dealing with prominent, endangered, extinct species from E. Bharucha. All the rest details in Bharucha would become repetitive and would lead to a loss of time. Also, go to the website of the Ministry of Environment and Forest and download the latest list of endangered species in India. This also contains the photographs of these organisms. It is recommended that the aspirants must specifically look at these photographs. Questions may be asked pertaining to the minute physical differences among these endangered species. In the present paper, the weightage of pollution-related questions decreased while that of ecology increased compared to that in the previous year. Questions on pollution were from predictable areas, while those from ecology were a little tricky this time. By reading the last unit of environment and ecology from NCERT class 12th biology book and the selected chapters of the Teachers' handbook on the environment, an aspirant could have solved 8 questions out of 20 asked in the paper. Extra efforts are required to crack other questions; Global programs/

initiatives regarding wetland protection, forest and biological diversity conservation are required to be studied in detail from the website of UNEP, UNDP, UNFCCC etc. The framework of our national laws in this direction needs to be looked into.

Science and technology: Let us divide science and technology into 2 parts. The first would deal with the traditional concepts of physics, chemistry, and biology, and the other aspect would consist of the current advances in scientific theories and technological breakthroughs. The humanities students may not feel scared of science as the level of understanding required is up to 10th level. The aspirants are required to go through the basic concepts of science given in NCERT class VI, VII, VIII exhaustively. As far as the NCERT class IX and X standard textbooks are concerned, we need to be highly selective in our efforts, which should be synchronous to the requirements. The physics and the chemistry content of class IX and X are not required for civil services. However, the chapter on light in class X dealing with reflection, refraction, and dispersion is to be studied minus the mathematical details related to it.

The second aspect deals with the current related science and technology news. The factual details will not be asked by UPSC. But while dealing with the current related events, the underlying principles have to be delineated from the information. The best way is to deliberate and reflect on that news which you have collected in your separate diary devoted to this purpose while reading the newspaper. Also, the *science reporter* magazine is a great source of awareness of recent advances in the field of S&T. It is, however, difficult to read each and every issue thoroughly as it involves too many factual details. An aspirant may replace the *science reporter* with *The Gist*, which contains the concise news of the science reporter. But do not read both.

Economics: This is one of the most interesting subjects in civil services preparations. It is because one can relate to this subject the current happenings in India and the world. Also, the fundamentals of economics are prevalent in the capitalistic outlook, which has taken roots in most parts of the contemporary world. Thus, a basic understanding of fundamentals is a prerequisite for an exhaustive study at national and international levels.

An aspirant is advised to start the journey with a thorough reading of economics NCERT textbooks of classes IX, X, XI, and XII. Here, the class XI microeconomics can be easily skipped and doesn't require discussion at all. On the contrary, the macroeconomics book of class XII is the cornerstone of civil services preliminary exam, dealing with money, banking and finance, the role of RBI, public finance, and related deficits. A second reading of this book would also not be considered a waste of effort as these concepts are majorly required for the mains examination as well. Once these basic necessary texts are covered, an aspirant may enjoy reading the economics and business section of the newspaper.

Although the foundation will be laid by NCERT textbooks in economics, these won't suffice your knowledge to tackle all the questions of the preliminary examination. The vacuum can be filled by coaching notes which deal with matters not elaborated in NCERTs, such as development indicators, money and capital markets, International monetary bodies, International trade, and finance. In CSAT 2014, one of the easiest parts of paper 1 was economics. The NCERT textbook of class 12th macroeconomics was sufficient to answer most of the questions. However, an aspirant is not advised to restrict to only one book as the study of economics is required for detailed analysis of many questions in mains. Some people were also disappointed to see such an easy level of economics!

Current Affairs: These questions came as a surprise for many. Direct facts were asked in the paper. Many aspirants compared this paper with that asked in common graduate level of SSC. However, the comparison is not justified merely on the introduction of 9 current affairs questions. The questions were related to places/countries in recent news which could not have missed the eye of serious aspirants. Also, one who has studied the schemes (highlighted in the box) in the economics survey must have not found any difficulty for scheme-related questions. For major flagship schemes, 3 things are required to be known for every scheme – funding ratios of Center & state, nodal ministry/agency, and the target audience. Overall, if an aspirant has not answered 6 questions out of 9 correctly, then there seems to be a problem in reading the newspaper. He/she must refer to the chapter on the role of newspaper, magazine, and website in the book. Note that no current affairs package of any coaching is required for answering these questions. Referring to packages of Vajiram for current related developments would unnecessarily create a burden of not required facts.

◈ Consolidated Strategy for Preliminary 2025

Taking into account the above considerations, I present to you a combined strategy of preliminary 2025, provided that the pattern of examination remains the same or doesn't change much. Assuming that an aspirant settles down by 15th September 2024 and the CSAT 2025 is scheduled in the month of August 2025, an aspirant is provided a time frame of at least 10 months, and the same has been constructively used to lay down the strategic study path to crack preliminary 2025 in the following manner;

Year/ Month	Important dates	What to do
2024 Sept	1st week	The thought of civil services must be conceived in the mind. 1. Analyzing that thought, introspecting for the reasons to join civil services. Talk to people selected, as well as studying. Ask about their reasons for studying for civil services. Try to develop a long-term vision – what will civil services give you? This can be realized by searching for the job profile of every service that fills the post through Civil Services Examination and trying to develop an opinion as to which service is synchronous with your needs and expectations. Remember, your interview preparation has begun. *(Read The decision to go for civil services.)* 2. If you decide to go for GS coaching, then search for that coaching whose timings suit your needs. Ideally, it should not be more than 3 hours in a day and a maximum of 4 days a week. 3. Do not rush into studies hastily and abruptly. Be patient. Speak less and lend an ear to listen. 4. Don't be in any hurry to finalize the optional. 5. Start reading the newspaper whenever you are free, not as a part of study, but as a source of entertainment. Do not be disheartened if you cannot make sense of some news. Leave it and move on. Do this for 15 days and get familiar with the types of sections the newspaper has.

2024 September	15th – 30th	1. If you want to take coaching for GS, then finalize it before the end of September. 2. If you have decided not to join, then refrain from joining coaching after September. 3. Create 5 small diaries, one each for polity, economics, social issues, environment/ science & technology, and international relations. The relevant news must be segregated and entered into the respective diary. (*Read the art of reading a newspaper in Chapter 3*)
2024 October	Full month	1. Whether you join coaching or not, an aspirant must be thorough with 2 GS subjects in the month of October. At least, the basic text must be complete. (*Read above – subject-wise analysis for the basic texts*) 2. Best combinations of 2 subjects to start off would be – (Polity + Economics) and (History + Geography). Avoid taking up science and technology in the beginning. 3. For this whole month of October, start thinking about the optional subject. Consider whether to opt for coaching for the optional subject or not, and if so, identify the best coaching that can work in sync with the ongoing GS classes (if any). These issues and more need to be resolved by the end of October. (*Read more on deciding the optional subject in Chapter 2.*)
2024 November	1st week	1. The optional subject, along with coaching (if any), must be finalized. 2. Two GS subjects must have been completed by now.

2024 November	Rest of the month	1. Now, the 3 tasks are continuous; firstly, the newly decided optional subject is a new entrant to the study. Thus, it has to be given a major chunk of your time. 2. Secondly, along with the optional, only one GS subject can be managed in tandem. Take any suitable subject of GS, preferably the one that continues in coaching. 3. Thirdly, by now you should be thorough with the smart reading techniques of the newspaper. Here, this technique will save at least one hour daily, which would prove beneficial in accommodating the extra optional subject. 4. Be immune to any controversy regarding the scrapping of optional subjects, if any.
2024 December	Full month	1. By the end of the year, an aspirant must be through with 3 GS subjects, good progress should have been made in the realms of the optional subject, and newspaper study time should not exceed one hour.
2025 Jan, Feb, Mar, April, May	Watch for the Notification of CSE, 2025	1. By the arrival of the notification, an aspirant should have completed the 3 GS subjects remaining. 2. The aspirant must have progressed through more than half of the optional subject. 3. Continuous reading of the monthly magazine 'Yojana' from January 2015. 4. In this period, another newspaper should be introduced on consecutive days. For example, an aspirant may read The Hindu one day and the very next day switch to The Indian Express, and then again to The Hindu on the third day. The same strategy is applicable to Hindi students who can read 2 Hindi newspapers in tandem. This leads to the incorporation of diverse views in both your analysis and the segregated diaries of different subjects.

		5. In the month of May, an aspirant must consider whether or not a test series is required for CSAT. If yes, a coaching institute that has relevant papers (according to the pattern and difficulty level of that of CSE) must be selected for Test series supplements.
2025 June	1st week	1. The coaching classes for GS and for the optional subject must be brought to a halt, whether the course over there is pending or not. Now is not the time for coaching, but only for self-study. 2. Study of the optional subject must be completely discontinued. 3. A decision must have been taken by now, whether or not a test series for CSAT from any coaching is required. 4. The first CSAT paper, whether you give it in coaching or at your premises, should be taken without any preparations. This is utmost necessary to identify your weakness – the critical areas – aspirants are required to work on these rather than deliberating on the whole course. 5. The 1st week of June shall also see the end of newspapers and the entry of analysis or facts in the diaries.
2025 June	2nd, 3rd, or 4th week	1. Focus on improving comprehension of paper 2 of GS by using newspapers. Write a summary of any one article from a newspaper within 6 to 8 minutes. The summary should be approximately one-third of the length of the original article. Continue this practice for at least 15 days. 2. One revision of at least 3 subjects of GS must be completed within the last 3 weeks of the month of June.

		3. Every alternate week, one complete CSAT paper must be given to analyze the performance. A list of weak topics must be prepared for both Paper 1 and Paper 2. 4. If the CSAT paper is taken in the comfort of your room or house, the time frame should be shortened by 10 minutes; that is, the maximum time allowed should be 1 hour and 50 minutes only.
2025 July	Full month	1. The month of July should be dedicated to revising the remaining 3 subjects in GS. 2. This has to be maintained with the continuity of taking CSAT papers at least once a week.
2025 August	Crash pre – 2024	1. The part of this month available before pre-2015 is critical. 2. This half-month or so is dedicated to attacking weaknesses, which have been compiled into a list by taking several CSAT papers earlier. 3. Frequency of CSAT papers must be increased to twice a week. The goal for this part of the month is to stabilize the score at around 110 for paper 1. Because the papers of coaching institutes are tougher than those of the actual CSAT examination of UPSC, the score in the exam would generally increase from what an aspirant maintains in the coaching test series or at home. 4. The timing of the papers must be adjusted so that a candidate does not take any paper 4 days before the preliminary examination.

2025	Day of pre – 2025	1. After the examination, an aspirant must not be apprehensive about his/her performance. Also, indolence or tiredness must not come in the way of checking the solutions released by the coaching institutes. To know your performance, whatever it may be, and its assessment is critical for planning the very next move. The variation in the scores assessed by solutions of coaching institutes and the actual score may not differ by 5 percent.

Countering Failure in Csat

From a genuine media source, I found that;

More than 4.5 lakh candidates appeared at the preliminary 2014 examination. A total of 9,44,926 candidates had applied for the examination, but only 6,80,455 downloaded the admit cards. Out of almost 7 lakh candidates, 4.5 lakh came for the test held at 2,137 centers in 59 cities. In the year 2013, the UPSC Civil services preliminary saw 3,24,101 candidates.

In the year 2015, the figure of appeared candidates is expected to be about 4.7 lacs. However, as there is no official declaration, there might be a possibility that even more candidates sat the exam, as the candidates who appeared in 2011 (2.5 lacs) had been given another chance in the year 2015.

Thus, let us consider an average of 5 lakh students who compete for around the first 15,000 ranks. The rest are not eligible to write the mains exams. This section is dedicated to all those aspirants who could not make it to the mains. I have tried to delineate the reasons for failure, the immediate strategy after the result, and the corrections which shall benefit the aspirant in the long run.

❖ **Unpredictable CSAT:**

CSAT, 2014, again reinforced our belief in the unpredictability of UPSC question-setting trends! It was notified through the Gazette that the marks of those comprehensions for which there was no Hindi translation were not to be considered in merit for the purpose of selection in CSAT. But surprises were far from being over.

The CSAT paper II again tricked many. It remains to be the prime cause of woes for several aspirants. The twist in this paper was the deletion of decision-making questions. But that was not realized by many aspirants until they searched for the decision-making questions and were terrified not to find them in the question booklet. Why worried if there was no decision-making? Because that is a section which can be traversed in a matter of a few minutes, and also, there is no negative marking. Thus, it is that section which boosts the score by 10-15 marks. Now it was not there.

In CSAT 2015, this paper 2 was made qualifying. People cheered, especially those who had been agitating for the scrapping of this paper entirely. A sort of compromise was reached, and there has been no protest since then. But even after that, 3 of my acquaintances, who had good know-how of GS, couldn't secure more than 33% in paper 2. Maybe because they became so complacent after the notification that no effort was put into this paper at all.

❖ **Missing the instructions:**

The suspicion should have been aroused in the minds of the aspirants upon reading the instructions at the first hand. Nowhere was it mentioned that there shall be some questions with no negative marking – both in the year 2014 as well as 2015. That should have been enough to attract attention of the aspirants directly to the decision-making questions. He/she should have known within 2 minutes after receiving the question paper that there are no decision-making questions. The consequential thought then must have been, "The paper is going to be lengthier." With this thought in mind, an aspirant should have proceeded with the paper. However, many candidates approached me after the paper with the grievance that they realized only after one hour into the exam that there was no decision-making section.

❖ **Two reasons for failure in CSAT:**

There can only be 2 reasons for a negative result in CSAT: a) Lack of subject knowledge and b) Lack of exam time temperament. The former can be managed by taking a deeper plunge into the studies, while the latter is indeed a cause for worry.

The irony is that most of the students had sufficient subject knowledge required for this year's CSAT, but it was the temperament in the exam and time management that mattered the most in this preliminary exam, which was not cultivated by many aspirants. Hence, the dismal results for them. The important thing is to realize that this temperament of handling pressure is not innate; it has to be nurtured, learned, and practiced.

One aspirant who was rendered hopeless after CSAT paper II vomited bluntly, "I just don't have the talent to crack CSAT. It's just not inside me." He burst into tears. At that time, I didn't find it appropriate to convince him of the gross error he had made while labeling the paper-solving talents as something innate in a human being. Nevertheless, through this book, I must convey to all the aspirants that question-solving techniques, time management tricks, and the related qualities can be learned and have to be cultivated if we are to succeed in CSAT in the present times.

❖ **Immediate course of action after failure:**

After writing the CSAT paper, a reasonable step would be to check your answers with those of coaching institutes. You will definitely get an idea of your score. Insecurity arises for those aspirants who are on the borderline of the expected cut-offs. They would usually check their answers with that of various coaching institutes in the hopes of getting one or 2 more questions correct. Planning the study for mains is a difficult course of action for such aspirants due to the insecurity of selection in the preliminary.

Once the result is out, we have only 2 cases: those who are through and those who have failed. The unsuccessful aspirants are bound to undergo a little torture in myriad forms. They would be anguished by the advice of different sections of society. Their friends who passed the preliminary would try to point out the mistakes they had made and share their experience. This might prove to be a good exercise, provided that the guiding friend does not pursue such advice with a humiliating intent. Another flawed methodology adopted is the formation of a consequential group of unsuccessful aspirants that gets created to share the burdens of defeat.

Parents and other family members may turn a little skeptical and start doubting the aspirant's capabilities. They won't say it directly but through words directed in such regard. That indeed is painful. One of my good friends who missed the preliminary by less than 10 marks was bestowed with suggestions of meditation by her father. *"My father said meditation and yoga can take me out of grief in times of failure. He also advised me to read motivational books."* My dear friends, the failure in CSAT is not to be projected as a 'grief' in our lives! Life is too long, dynamic, and versatile that an unsuccessful examination result can't and should not be labeled as an invincible grief in our lives. Taking the above view into account, I present below a broad strategy to counter the failure in CSAT;

1. **Take a break** – There may develop immense pressure, both from internal expectations and external comments, that an aspirant may take to study on the day he/she witnesses the negative result in CSAT. This pressure to study is not going to help. What is required at that moment is profound introspection into what went wrong. Delineating the cause of failure is a must for each and every aspirant. "Take a break" means to give a breather from studies. It does not necessarily mean that you have to go to the Himalayas for a vacation. What it implies is that you may speak less and introspect more.

    Is it the lack of drive within you that resulted in fewer efforts, which resulted in failure? If yes, then you may search for your reasons for doing civil services preparations, which will help you find that vigor in your studies. Or is it the exam time pressure that you could not handle while writing the paper? These questions and more need to be answered before you proceed to studies again. It may take you 15 or 20 days to rejuvenate your energies and have more clarity in your mind regarding the reasons for preparations and your weaknesses in CSAT. But this is a must – do not think that these 20 days were wasted. In fact, introspection after a failure leads to more profound planning to attain the target. This indeed will take time but would go a long way!

2. **Isolate negativities** – Try to discern the intent of the friends around you while you are engulfed by the failure in CSAT. There will be those who would approach you with a smile on their face, humbleness, and calmness in their voice. They may criticize you to correct you. However, they will not mock at you and amplify your pain of failure.

   While others, far greater in number generally, would be those who try to humiliate you by their comments. It is far more beneficial to leave the company of such creatures for the moment, rather than losing your precious energies to counter their arguments. They would never give up their reasons and contentions as it is just not their purpose to come to a conclusive talk. Distinguish and isolate these mundane creatures!

3. **How to mitigate 2 or more consecutive failures** – UPSC Civil services preparations is a bloody vicious circle. There is an easy entry into this circle but exit is quite difficult to create. Just recall the working of a stock trader or a mutual fund. There are 2 well-known instruments – hedging the risk and stop loss function. Use both these instruments in your civil services preparations so as to minimize the losses, if any. Hedge the risk, that is, play safe. Keep on filling the forms of such examinations that are closely related to the civil services course content.

Secondly, put an upper limit on the number of unsuccessful attempts of CSAT. I personally feel that 2 consecutive failed attempts at CSAT are a signal that something is terribly wrong with your strategy, in which a lack of knowledge is most probably not the reason. Moreover, a third failed attempt of CSAT calls for quitting the preparations. That is indeed a difficult thing to write in this book and even more painful to realize. But it is a pragmatic thought that life must not be brought to a standstill. At some point in time, we have to make life move on. This is further elaborated in myths and FAQs.

❖ **Long-term course of action after failure:**

While planning the strategy of preliminary for the next year, one must closely analyze the CSAT paper and try to discern the intent of UPSC. The examination focuses more on managing your time rather than testing your in-depth knowledge. Aspirants with tremendous knowledge of GS didn't gain much in paper I as much as they lost in paper II if they were slow, lethargic, or inefficient in their time management strategies.

The question is, why so much stress on efficient time management? Why is UPSC not setting paper-I with difficult theoretical questions from the subject matter, that is, from history, polity, etc.? Because the bureaucrats in the contemporary times have to be quick in taking decisions. With so much accessibility to information at the hands of everyone, its analysis and inferences based on that analysis occupy the prime position rather than just knowing or learning the information. Further, in the complex world we live in, multi-tasking is bound to increase with the proliferation of information and its accessibility. A civil servant has to be versatile. In this regard, a civil servant may be equated with the senior managerial position in the corporate sector; the only difference being that the former works for the government machinery, which itself is huge and linked intimately with the civil society, media, household, international domain, and so on.

Thus, in this complex world, apart from land, labor, and capital, time has become an equally important resource in managing the functions of not only the corporates but also the government sector. This is reflected in the question papers for the selection of the backbone of the government machinery, the civil services. Therefore, my dear friends, it is better to acknowledge the demands of present times rather than criticizing the skewed question-setting trend as perceived by many aspirants. It is better to accept the lack of efficient time management skills and work upon it rather than continuing your preparations in an obsolete fashion. The following broad guidelines are presented in this regard;

1. **Reading v/s scanning** – When sitting at the comfort of our homes, we read newspapers, NCERTs, or any other study material without calculating our reading speed. Why? Because grasping the concept is more important than just completing the chapter, article, or essay within a time limit. Indeed justified. However, the same habit plays a negative role when answering the comprehension section in the CSAT paper II. If you have tried to solve the comprehension part of paper 2 of CSAT, you will realize that the speed for a single reading would not be less than 100 words per minute. And believe me, dear aspirants, this paper specifically intends that candidates must not read the passage twice to answer questions. This requires not just reading skills but scanning through the content.

   Read fast enough so that the basic idea is imprinted into the mind before you move on to the questions related to the passage. The imprint should be strong enough that you minimize the need to look back at the passage again. Now this skill need not be innate, but it can be cultivated. Each day, read just one article of any newspaper very fast, that is, within a time limit such that you must read 100 words per minute. After reading, the aspirant must write down the summary of that passage in not more than one-third of the original number of words. This practice is not related to the study of GS part. Please demarcate one passage or article for this solemn task daily. Further, those articles demarcated must cover different areas, such as ecology, science, politics, and international affairs, and so on, so that you are conversant with the topics of various areas. Do this for at least a month and then start taking the CSAT mock papers of any coaching institutes.

2. **Work under pressure** – In the year 2008, my college junior had no hope for himself regarding his career. He suffered from extreme lethargy and was forced to resign from a construction firm in 2010. He wandered around for a year doing odd jobs. In 2011, he took the CAT exam and somehow managed to secure a 99.99 percentile, leading to his admission to IIM Ahmedabad. I met him in 2013, just after my CSE mains in December, and I was surprised to see the formerly lazy character replaced by aggression, a sharp mindset, and a diplomatic approach.

"It seems you have undergone a mental surgical transformation. What did they do to you in IIM?" I posed a natural question upon witnessing this amazing event. "They make us work under pressure, tremendous pressure. In IIMs, they made us used to handle pressure and find the delicate balance between competing pursuits," he answered honestly.

I could very well relate to what pressure he was talking about. Dear aspirants, UPSC Civil services are an exam of tremendous pressure. Right from CSAT to the mains and till the interview, you would be grilled in different pressure situations and still be expected to remain calm and composed, and moreover, take decisions.

Thus, before actually facing such stressful exams, you must get into daily practice of stretching your limits – both mental and physical. You must set yourself a task that would push your limits.

In this regard, the section dealing with *calculating the number of hours of study* and *the role of the calendar*, discussed in the last chapter, is important. Test series, both for preliminaries and mains, are also important tools to simulate exam-like conditions if taken seriously.

3. **Cultivate some passion, skill, or talent** – The perception that a civil servant is one who is into the books all the time, one who is a nerd or geek, and can only talk about concepts and theories is now obsolete and highly unfitting. The bureaucrats are smart people equaling, if not exceeding, the *'smartness quotient'* in the corporate sector. In the training, I realized that the civil servants recruited from diverse regions and different sections also come equipped with myriad interests and talents. These people can sing, dance, and act. Some of them are professionally into sports and had won past accolades. I was astonished to find diverse talents emanating from among the selected candidates of CSE. Some of my batch mates can play guitar and harmonium. One among us is an excellent *shayar*, and I am particularly impressed by his works in Hindi and Urdu both. Another fellow beat me in chess 3 times within 20 minutes, even though I do play chess well, but indeed he was much better and played professionally.

These skills, talents, or passions, apart from your mainstream duty, which apparently is studying for UPSC, make you a little more versatile. Look at what I am doing – writing. I had always wanted to be a writer. During the tenure of my preparations, I had also been working on a novel which is yet to be released. That remains my passion, and now I am nurturing it so that my works can see the light of day.

These kinds of additional skills will help you along during your preparations. These will provide you with the necessary breaks. Furthermore, these may serve as points of discussion in the interview as well. Interests and passions could be very diverse.

Some may be fond of movies, while others may like to sing or listen to songs. Take it to a level ahead – be a connoisseur of movies or songs – know inside and out what invokes your interest.

Some aspirants may put forth a valid argument that CSE preparations drain away a chunk of energy, leaving none to find or pursue one's interests or passions. True. Possessing additional skills is only an added advantage in certain situations, but never a necessary condition for selection. Although one must keep in mind that it is better to discover your interests and nurture them rather than wasting too much time on unproductive gossiping with friends.

Preparations for Mains Examination

The Civil Services Examination of 2013 witnessed a drastic change in the pattern of mains examination. Out of the 2 optional subjects, one was replaced by 2 additional papers of general studies. This increased the weightage of GS to twice that of the optional subject. Earlier, its weightage was half that of the 2 optional subjects combined. The number of questions in the GS papers was increased to 25 of 10 marks each, to be completed in 3 hours. The thinking time was reduced, and speed in writing answers mattered a lot. The intent behind this could have been to elicit a natural response from an aspirant rather than a cultivated one or the one that is administered by coaching/training – when faced with questions in the examination hall rapidly. Also, it was compulsory to score at least 10% of total marks in each of the 7 papers in mains examination to be considered for merit, that is, one essay, 4 GS papers, and 2 papers of an optional subject.

The course of all the 4 papers of general studies was explicitly listed in the notification of CSE 2013. An altogether new subject was introduced in general studies paper – IV called Ethics, Integrity and Aptitude. The introduction of this paper in GS signifies the importance attached to personal and professional ethics of civil servants by UPSC. The quality a civil servant must possess is discussed in the next chapter on 'preparations for interview.' Several, but not all, changes introduced in CSE 2013 were taken from the recommendation of the Arun Nigavekar committee report submitted in August 2012. The report is now available in the public domain by means of RTI.

It was contended before the committee that aspirants at such important positions of civil services generally qualify by scoring well in the 2 optional subjects, which would have no relevance to the services as such. The civil servants are employed in generalist or functionalist positions and are required to possess a broad general outlook on important current happenings. Taking into account these and other related views, the committee decided to scrap one optional subject and replace it with GS papers. Moreover, civil services preliminary examination served as a screening exam for Indian forest services in 2013. This had a significant repercussion on the decreased final merit cut-offs in the forest services.

However, there was no change in the compulsory language portion – one is English, and the other language can be opted from the list of 22 languages in schedule 8 of the constitution. The minimum qualifying standards are listed in the notification – 25% for both the Indian language and the English language. Marks of the interview have been decreased from 300 earlier to 275 in 2013, such that the percentage weightage of the interview in the total score for merit remains the same. These changes again provoked a huge uproar after the period of speculation of 2 months before the notification. To pacify the aspirants, the number of attempts for every category, where there was a limitation, was increased by 2 with a consequential increase in 2 years of the maximum age limit wherever applicable.

The pattern of the mains examination broadly remains the same in the year 2014. It is ironical that 2013 witnessed an uproar mainly due to drastic changes in the mains examination, and in the year 2014, it was the converse – protests surrounded the preliminary examination and not the mains examination! Let us try to devise a strategic plan to crack the mains of CSE. Let me assure you, dear aspirant, that mains are competitively easier than prelims just because of the numbers – out of the 16,000 selected candidates in the preliminary stage, around 3,000 would be selected on the basis of the subjective mains examination to face the interview. A well-chalked-out strategy that can organize your studies, recall to memory the information written in a structured manner, and examination hall temperament can definitely help you emerge in flying colors in the mains examination. All those aspirants who find the mains examination invincible, those who always get through the preliminary and then find mains as a bottleneck to crack open, and those who have believed till now that the mains examination is the only barrier between them and the civil services shall be beneficiaries of these nuances which are to follow in the sections below;

◈ ESSAY

Essay is nothing but a reflection of general studies. It is a broad, multi-faceted assessment of a particular topic under consideration from a generalist viewpoint – a quality mandatory for a civil servant to possess so as to deliberate upon important issues. From the point of view of examination, an essay exam is the one where you can create a difference in scores. The marks of an essay vary widely, and it will require certain skills to maintain your score in the range of average and above-average marks but profound strategy and practice to land up in the top range of marks. An essay has become more important in the present scenario where the knowledge difference among the aspirants as far as GS is concerned is minuscule; resulting in very closely spaced marks in GS. It is here that an essay can give you a huge lead from the competitors. Thus, after a lot of discussions and deliberation with the other successful candidates and their candid sharing of expected marks and actual scores, I have come to the following effective strategy for the essay;

a) Distinguish between areas and topics:

An aspirant needs to know the difference between an area and the topics falling in that area. For example, social issues are an area, and the topics falling in that area may be women empowerment, family values, casteism, etc. Another example – Environment is an area. The topics falling under that area are pollution of air, degradation of land, deforestation, erosion of coastal areas, etc. Thus, we can make out that an area is a broad domain incorporating many topics which are the subsets of that broad area.

Now an aspirant must recall the way of reading a newspaper – the art of smart reading of a newspaper – wherein entries are made into different diaries titled as social, economic, political, environmental, international relations, science & technology. These are nothing but the broad areas listed for you, and the entries therein may comprise material to be used in the relevant essays. That means the exercise an aspirant did for his/her general studies preparations by extracting and segregating news of relevance would also prove beneficial in the essay.

Remember, dear friends, that those essays which provide suitable, current, related examples, in accordance with the topic under consideration, create a tremendous effect on the examiner. This is bound to fetch more marks.

b) Make a list of your strong areas:

For the purpose of an essay, the number of areas swells by incorporating philosophical, historical, and cultural topics along with the existing lot of social, economic, political, IR, Environment, and S & T. An aspirant must identify his/her comfort zone. You must pick at least 3 areas of your comfort – when I talk of comfort, it includes the assumption that you are aware of the recent happenings related to that field. The fourth area is bound to be chosen to act as a buffer in case of contingency.

Analyze the essays of the last 3 years. You will realize that the topics of the essays find their roots in at least 2 areas and a maximum of 3 areas – except for the philosophical essays. Thus, an aspirant must select 3 areas of maximum comfort so that he/she has the information to build on and conclude the essay from those 3 areas.

Further, there must be either environment or science and technology in those 3 areas. These both areas are finding relevance in wide issues and can't be neglected in an essay. The best combination of robust areas would be social, economic, and science and technology, with the political area as a buffer. Another good combination would be economic, political, and environment, with the social area as a buffer to act for contingency. A buffer area means that when it doesn't find relevance to any one of the 3 core areas, then the buffer area can be plugged in.

After deciding the 3 core areas and the fourth buffer area, an aspirant must be thorough with the current happenings and their analysis in those areas.

c) Analysis of CSE 2015 (mains) essays:

An element of surprise in the civil services paper of UPSC is no surprise at all, at least in the last 3 or 4 years! The notification of 2014 CSE should have been paid heed, which read as below;

PAPER-I Essay: Candidates may be required to write essays on multiple topics. They will be expected to keep closely to the subject of the essay, to arrange their ideas in an orderly fashion, and to write concisely. Credit will be given for effective and exact expression.

The same is the language of the CSE 2015 notification.

"MULTIPLE TOPICS" – these words were sufficient to ring bells in the minds of an aspirant. And as it happened, there came 2 essays to be written in the paper; of course, the word limits were reduced to almost half of what they had been in the year 2013. The essays too were more restricted to a particular area of interest in their approach and content, and that too found their origins in burning hot current issues compared to what was presented in 2013. Let us see what CSE mains 2015 essays have to offer to the aspirants;

SECTION A

Topic of essay	Area 1	Area 2	Area 3	Buffer
Lending hands to someone is better than giving a dole.	Philosophy	Economic	Economic	International relations,
Quick, but steady, wins the race.	Philosophy	Economic	International relations	
The character of an institution is reflected in its leader.	Polity/ Political system	Economic	Social	Cultural
Education without values, as useful as it is, seems rather to make a man more clever devil.	Economic and social problems in current world	Ethics and values and Globalization effects on values	Human capital formation by education	Cultural

SECTION B

Topic of essay	Area 1	Area 2	Area 3	Buffer
Technology cannot replace manpower	Advances in S & T	Social	Economic	Environmental
Crisis faced in India – moral or economic.	Economic	Ethics and morality and values	Social and cultural	

Dreams that should not let India sleep.	Ideals of constitution.	Insecurities of India – economic, health, energy, food, water, etc.	International relations,	Environmental
Can capitalism bring inclusive growth?	Economic philosophy	Globalization/ liberalization and privatization	Social and cultural lag due to capitalism.	Environmental

The order of prominence of areas is decreasing from area 1 to the buffer area. This identification of the area around which the topic of the essay revolves, gradation of the importance of areas in that topic will help in the identification of the topic chosen to be written for the purpose of examination. An aspirant is advised to practice the above-said analysis of at least 3 other mains examination essays and thereafter discuss it with faculties prominent in this field.

a) Composition of an essay:

It is written in the question that an essay should not be more than 1200 words. It doesn't mean that you have to write as close as possible to the benchmark of 1200 words. Why? It is a 3-hour paper, is it so difficult to write a total of around 2500 words in 3 hours?

The answer lies in the notification for the CSE which tells the candidates to, "Arrange their ideas in an orderly fashion and to write concisely." This arrangement or sequencing of *thoughts* would take time and would not happen if an aspirant just takes to writing the moment he/she is given the question-cum-answer booklet. In fact, it is advice to the dear aspirant that he/she should invest at least half an hour and a maximum of 45 minutes to prepare the blueprint of an essay, and the remaining time should be spent writing the sentences to constitute the essay. Thus, the effective time to write down the essay has reduced from 3 hours to 2 hours (max) or 1.5 hours (min). From my own experience of writing and reading several blogs on human speed of writing in different circumstances, especially those which invite thinking, the speed can be approximately 18 words per minute. Thus, the number of words that can be written in 1.5 hours would be 1620, and that in 2 hours would be 2160. Thus, I consider an approximate average of both the values to be 2000 to be the optimum number of words that should compose both the essays. Thus, taking a variance of 50 words, 950 to 1050 would be sufficient number of words written for each of the 2 essays.

These 1000 or so words would be spread into 3 parts of an essay: introduction, body, and conclusion. The introduction will generally consist of 130 words divided into 2 paragraphs which would introduce the topic of the essay to the examiner. This may be done with the help of definitions of basic concepts overtly expressed by the essay or hidden in its essence. The conclusion will generally be of 120 words and would present a forward-looking approach and an aspirant's vision for the country in context with the subject of the essay. In this regard, thoroughly go with the approach of Yojana to every issue, challenge, or problem faced by the country. It is never pessimistic in its approach throughout. Never have I seen nihilistic opinions aired by the authors. The conclusive paragraphs must not be more than 2, but these should be highly visionary and forward-looking.

Why? Because a civil servant, if pessimistic, would negate the spirit of public service itself. It is not that problems and challenges would not be encountered in pragmatic situations, but it is the character of a civil servant to face these challenges as an opportunity for the betterment of his/her countrymen. That aspect must be reflected in your essay. This character of yours as a pragmatic trouble-shooter, within the domains of law, with a vision and foresight, is utmost important. This has to be reflected in your conclusion of the essay.

b) The blueprint and the body of the essay:

The body of an essay, constituting around 750 words, is the main analysis of the topic of the essay and would be based on the blueprint thoroughly prepared by the candidate in at least half an hour devoted to it. To prepare a blueprint, an effective way is to use the division chart of the topic of the essay – detailing the areas it touches. The points coming to mind should be written in the relevant area. "A candidate is expected to keep closely to the subject of the essay," says the notification of CSE 2014. The thoughts coming to your mind may not be related closely to the subject matter; nevertheless, write them down at first. These will be filtered in the second process of organizing and sequencing. At first, these may not be linked or organized but may be written in a random fashion. Remember, the thoughts won't flash in your mind in a sequenced flow generally, but these would be abrupt flashes. This is the most significant but highly tormenting part of the blueprint. Sometimes, an aspirant may feel that none is emerging in his/her mind and this may incite a thought to switch over to another essay. But, dear aspirant, you have to eliminate this treacherous tendency. Because once you have selected the essay according to your areas of comfort, the thoughts are bound to come to your mind. It is here that you have to persevere, maintain your calm, have faith in your judgment of the essay and stick to it.

In this exercise, what would add as a supplement booster will be the current facts and analysis of the newspaper, which has been segregated into well-maintained diaries. It is easier to recall these facts related to the essay and list them in the relevant area which composes the essay.

Once this exercise is done, the next step is to get these random thoughts into a well-organized pattern. There cannot be listed any explicit rule that can be used by an aspirant to organize random thoughts into one of cause and effect, but it is only a matter of practice that mastery of this art can be achieved. With the blueprint ready, the body is only an extrapolation of that blueprint in the essay by making sentences and connecting these sentences with connectors.

◈ GS PAPER 1: Indian Heritage and Culture, History and Geography of the World and Society

This is the most static and predictable paper in the mains examination, and thus, the potential for a good score is high. However, it would require a significant part of effort on behalf of an aspirant to have a good command of History and Geography of both India and the world. The reason is simple – the course content is huge. Also, the numbers of questions in 2015 were reduced from 25 to 20 questions of 12.5 marks each.

Here I will tell you how to build upon the knowledge of History and Geography that has already been acquired to some extent while studying for the preliminary examination. What minimum incremental effort is required over and above the already existing base of prelims to maximize the score in this paper? The analysis of the paper in 2015 and answer writing techniques have also been delved into.

Analysis of the GS paper 1 in CSE (Mains), 2015:

Course content	Questions in CSE Mains 2015 and percentage weightage	Additional readings (over and above preliminary preparations)
Indian culture will cover salient aspects of art forms, literature, and architecture from ancient to medieval times.	The ancient civilisation in the Indian sub-continent differed from those of Egypt, Mesopotamia, and Greece in that its culture and traditions have been preserved without a breakdown to the present day. Comment.	The questions were from known topics but not direct; instead, they were anticipatory and inference-based. The weightage of this section has increased from 8% in CSE 2013 to presently 10%. The readings for this section must include NCERT Class XII 'Themes in Indian history,' Parts 1, 2, and 3. Selective readings of Bhakti

	Mesolithic rock-cut architecture of India not only reflects the cultural life of the times but also a fine aesthetic sense comparable to modern painting. Critically evaluate this comment. ... 10% weightage.	and Sufi movements, colonial cities are required. As the questions in this section are inference-based, very detailed coaching notes won't be required as these are not the need of the hour. (Refer to the special section of art and culture at the end of this chapter)
Modern Indian history from about the middle of the eighteenth century until the present – significant events, personalities, and issues. The Freedom Struggle – its various stages and important contributors/ contributions from different parts of the country.	How different would the achievement of Indian independence have been without Mahatma Gandhi? Discuss. Mahatma Gandhi and Dr B.R. Ambedkar, despite having divergent approaches and strategies, shared a common goal of ameliorating the downtrodden. Elucidate. It would have been difficult for the Constituent Assembly to complete its historic task of drafting the Constitution for Independent India in just 3 years, but for the experience gained with the Government of India Act, 1935. Discuss. ....15% weightage	The questions from modern Indian history are not particularly direct in their content and intent. A basic reading of the text 'History of Modern India' by Bipin Chandra along with NCERT Class VIII textbooks, 'Our Past – III,' both part 1 and 2, is required. However, there is absolutely no requirement to read 'India's Struggle for Independence' by the same author as it is an exhaustive detailed study that won't be necessary to answer questions at the civil services level in the present-day scenario.
Post-independence consolidation and reorganization within the country.		

History of the world will include events from the 18th century, such as the industrial revolution, world wars, redrawal of national boundaries, colonization, decolonization, and political philosophies like communism, capitalism, socialism, etc. – their forms and effects on society.	Why did the Industrial Revolution first occur in England? Discuss the quality of life of the people there during industrialization. How does it compare with that in India at present? To what extent can Germany be held responsible for causing the 2 World Wars? Discuss critically. … 10% weightage.	Although the weightage of world history has decreased from 16% in 2013 to 10% currently, the topic itself remains important and should spark inevitable interest in the aspirant's mind. The questions do not delve into the nuances of specific world events but focus on the broad causes and their probable effects on the world. The reading should include the basic texts of NCERT Class IX and X titled 'India and the Contemporary World' parts 1 and 2, along with Section IV – 'Toward Modernization' of Class XII NCERT – 'Themes in World History.' The extensive notes from coaching institutes such as Vajiran would only be a futile read; instead, notes by Himanshu Khatri, sir, can be referred to as a concise substitute.
Salient features of Indian Society, Diversity of India.	Describe any 4 cultural elements of diversity in India, and rate their relative significance in building a national identity. …… 5% weightage	Such general questions, if explained through concepts, would prove to be a better answer. For this, some basic theoretical understanding of society may be extracted from the NCERT Class XI textbook 'Understanding Society' first 2 chapters and the NCERT Class XII textbook 'Indian Society' chapters 1, 2, 3, and 6.

Role of women and women's organizations, population and associated issues, poverty and developmental issues, urbanization, their problems, and their remedies.	Critically examine whether a growing population is the cause of poverty, OR if poverty is the main cause of population increase in India. How do you explain the statistics that show the sex ratio in tribes in India is more favorable to women than the sex ratio among Scheduled Castes? Discuss the changes in the trends of labor migration within and outside India in the last 4 decades. Mumbai, Delhi, and Kolkata are the 3 mega cities of the country, but air pollution is a much more serious problem in Delhi compared to the other 2. Why is this so? Smart cities in India cannot sustain without smart villages. Discuss this statement in the backdrop of rural-urban integration. ... 25% weightage	Basic text that can be referred to is NCERT Class XII textbook 'Social change and development in India,' chapters 4 and 5. This can be strengthened by additional readings of some good coaching notes such as those of RIAS or Vajiram – both are adept in this regard.
Effects of globalization on Indian society.	Discuss the positive and negative effects of globalization on women in India. ... 5% weightage.	It is better not to search and read for specific text on this general topic, as your articulated answer from a general understanding would suffice for the requirements.

Social empowerment, communalism, regionalism, and secularism.	Debate the issue of whether and how contemporary movements for the assertion of Dalit identity work toward the annihilation of caste. ..... 5% weightage	To answer this section, one must have the basic understanding of the concepts given in the NCERT Class XI political science textbook titled 'Political Theory.'
Salient features of the world's physical geography.	Explain the factors responsible for the origin of ocean currents. How do they influence regional climates, fishing, and navigation? .... 5% weightage	The questions this year consisted of typical air pressure systems of the earth. All such topics can be read from NCERT Class XI Textbook titled 'Fundamentals of Physical Geography.' In this regard, the geography book of Knowracle publication may also be referred.
Distribution of key natural resources across the world (including South Asia and the Indian sub-continent); factors responsible for the location of primary, secondary and tertiary sector industries in various parts of the world (including India).	India is well endowed with fresh water resources. Critically examine why it still suffers from water scarcity. The states of Jammu and Kashmir, Himachal Pradesh, and Uttarakhand are reaching the limits of their ecological carrying capacity due to tourism. Critically evaluate. What are the economic significances of the discovery of oil in the Arctic Sea and its possible environmental consequences? .....15% weightage	The weightage of this topic has increased from 12% in the year 2013 to 15% at present. It includes both India's economic geography and that of the world. The distribution of resources has been covered in the preliminary section, and for the world's natural resources, it may be covered in the study material of Vajiram. Nevertheless, the questions require application of mind, and it is advisable to refer to any good sample question papers on this topic in particular.

Important geophysical phenomena such as earthquakes, tsunami, volcanic activity, cyclones, etc., geographical features, their locations, changes in critical geographical features (including water bodies and ice caps), and in flora and fauna, and the effects of such changes.	How far do you agree that the behavior of the Indian monsoon has been changing due to humanizing landscapes? Discuss. ...... 5% weightage	Reading the above-written text will also cover this part. These concepts are not in isolation of the phenomena which have been discussed above.

Comments On GS Paper 1 Of CSE (Mains):

As we can see above, the study material for the paper is copious. Therefore, even if the paper is of a static nature, getting more than 80 marks is a task in itself. The part of art and culture should be made into notes, and at the end of the day, only these notes should be revised. However, there is no requirement to create notes of world history as the questions would be more analytical than factual. Thus, an aspirant must refrain from learning world history.

A girl studying from a reputed coaching institute came to me when 2 months were left before writing mains 2013. "I am stuck up in the American revolution," she said plainly. Upon digging deeper into the issue, I found that she was stuck in remembering the minute events, their chronology, and dates. "I just want to make my answer so perfect," that is what she replied when I asked her why. I tried my level best but could not eliminate from her that instinct of being the 'perfect one creating perfect answers.' After my result, I realized that she had dropped her idea of being an IPS, which she had coveted so much a few months back!

My point is that there is a general tendency of coaching institutes – due to the fierce competition with each other – that each wants to see itself as superior to the others. This is achieved by distinguishing the class notes from those of other coaching institutes through incorporating unnecessary and absolutely redundant facts. An aspirant must not be a victim of the mutual competition among institutes. Moving on to answer writing in Paper 1 of GS, the goal should not be to write the most perfect answer, but to write as many answers as possible with exact and precise expression. The paper will be so extensive that we will barely find time to remember details, nuances, and our grammar and language skills would play an almost redundant role.

For every 10-mark question, an aspirant has to write up to 160 words in the 2015 CSE. To write as close as possible to this maximum limit is not our target, but to write as close as possible to the demand of the question in the minimum possible time is our goal. Thus, I feel that 80% of the maximum prescribed word limit should be your target. The challenge here would be to attempt around 230 marks out of 250 total. Remember, my dear aspirant, the target is to maximize marks, not to write 3 or 4 perfect answers.

◈ GS PAPER 2: Governance, Constitution, Polity, Social Justice and International Relations

This paper is very dynamic in its essence. It will require continuous upgrades of current affairs, which need to be incorporated in the answers. The issue here is not its dynamic nature but overlapping content. Once we analyze the paper, we will find common areas between different topics. Therefore, we must be cautious of repetitive efforts that could lead to a waste of a lot of time.

Still, there exists some static part of the content in the form of constitution and polity. This is a scoring part and would cover up any deficit that is created in the marks due to a lack of knowledge in current affairs. Further, international relations, though dynamic, is another part where an aspirant can score very good marks. Here, the role of segregated newspaper notes will come into play, but compiling them would be a painstaking task.

Governance and social justice are overlapping in their essence and content and yet so wide that without structuring, these would create havoc until the last moment. Governance, particularly, would attract many general, looking questions. A candidate may be tempted to believe that these questions can be answered without sufficient knowledge of the content of governance. This tendency has to be evaded in paper 2. The common-sense subject matter has to be studied, filtered, and structured into organized notes. All this will be dealt with after the analysis of GS paper 2 in mains 2015.

Analysis of the GS paper 2 in CSE (Mains), 2015:

Course content	Questions in CSE Mains 2015 and percentage weightage	Additional readings (over and above preliminary preparations)
Indian Constitution – historical underpinnings, evolution, features, amendments, significant provisions, and basic structure.	Does the right to a clean environment entail legal regulations on burning crackers during Diwali? Discuss in the light of Article 21 of the Indian Constitution and judgments of the apex court in this regard. .... 5% weightage	The questions are far from direct. It is not required to memorize the details of how the constitution emerged – a part of which is also common with history. The first few chapters of Laxmikant cater to this section.

Functions and responsibilities of the Union and the States, issues and challenges pertaining to the federal structure, devolution of powers and finances up to local levels, and challenges therein.	Discuss the possible factors that inhibit India from enacting, for its citizens, a uniform civil code as provided for in the Directive Principles of State Policy. Discuss The concept of cooperative federalism has been increasingly emphasized in recent years. Highlight the drawbacks in the existing structure and the extent to which cooperative federalism would address the shortcomings. In the absence of a well-educated and organized local-level government system, 'Panchayats' and 'Samitis' have remained mainly political institutions and not effective instruments of governance. Critically discuss. ... 15% weightage	Although the question from this section was direct, this section requires in-depth knowledge of all aspects of center-state relations – administrative, legislative, and financial. Discussions and debate on federalism are evolving, so aspirants are requested to read this from Subhash Kashyap and NCERT Class XI textbook. Local government and related provisions may be studied from Laxmikant.
Separation of powers between various organs, dispute redressal mechanisms, and institutions.	Khap Panchayats have been in the news for functioning as extra-constitutional authorities, often delivering pronouncements amounting to human rights violations. Discuss critically the actions taken by the legislative, executive, and the judiciary to set things right in this regard. ......5% weightage	This section deals with the delicate balance of executive, legislature, and judiciary. The structure and functionality of the higher judiciary need to be studied in detail. The alternate dispute redressal mechanism also needs mention here. Deliberation of constitutional, statutory, regulatory, and quasi-judicial bodies are well presented in Laxmikant.

Comparison of the Indian constitutional scheme with that of other countries.		Question from this section is unlikely. However, the features our constitution has borrowed from different constitutions of other countries must be known. One small chapter in Laxmikant deals with this.
Parliament and State Legislatures – structure, functioning, conduct of business, powers, privileges, and issues arising out of these.		This section is well-drafted in the book written by Subhash Kashyap, 'Our Constitution.' For the conduct rules, one may refer to the Lok Sabha website as well. If we look at both the mains of 2013 and 2014, the questions from this section try to extract an aspirant's problem-solving capacity rather than just the facts stated in the articles. In this regard, the package of Sriram, 'Indian Constitution, Polity and Governance,' tries to bring out the underlying polity of the burning hot current topics.
Structure, organization, and functioning of the Executive and the Judiciary Ministries and Departments of the Government; pressure groups, and formal/ informal associations, and their role in the Polity.		
Salient features of the Representation of People's Act.		Vajiram mains package has sufficiently covered the RPA, along with the Supreme Court judgments, in its interpretations.

Appointment to various constitutional posts, powers, functions, and responsibilities of various constitutional bodies.	Resorting to ordinances has always raised concern regarding the violation of the spirit of the separation of powers doctrine. While noting the rationales justifying the power to promulgate ordinances, analyze whether the decisions of the Supreme Court on the issue have further facilitated resorting to this power. Should the power to promulgate ordinances be repealed? .... 5% weightage	President, Vice President, Governor, CAG, Attorney General, judges of SC and HC, and Finance Commission are the main stress areas here. Comparative charts mentioning the qualifications, powers, emoluments, privileges, removal, etc., are suggested to be made from Laxmikant.
Statutory, regulatory, and various quasi-judicial bodies.	What are the major changes brought in the Arbitration and Conciliation Act, 1996 through the recent Ordinance promulgated by the President? How far will it improve India's dispute resolution mechanism? Discuss. "For achieving the desired objectives, it is necessary to ensure that the regulatory institutions remain independent and autonomous." Discuss in the light of the experiences in recent past. .... 10% weightage	This is very well given at the end of Laxmikant. Yet, apart from those mentioned in the standard text, one should be vigilant of any other new statutory or regulatory body being debated in current news and its proposed mandate.

Government policies and interventions for development in various sectors, and issues arising out of their design and implementation.		The proposal of the budget each year has to be studied in detail to gauge the policy changes in various sectors, specifically in trade-related issues. Once these changes have been listed, an aspirant should consult expert teachers to elicit the challenges, as well as the effects of implementation.
Development processes and the development industry – the role of NGOs, SHGs, various groups and associations, donors, charities, institutional, and other stakeholders.	Examine critically the recent changes in the rules governing foreign funding of NGOs under the Foreign Contribution (Regulation) Act (FCRA), 1976. The Self-Help Group (SHG) Bank Linkage Program (SBLP), which is India's own innovation, has proved to be one of the most effective poverty alleviation and women empowerment programs. Elucidate. How can the role of NGOs be strengthened in India for development works relating to the protection of the environment? Discuss, throwing light on the major constraints. .... 15% weightage	This section broadly accommodates the structure, issues, and linkages of various voluntary organizations. National policy on voluntary organizations must be studied from the internet. More details are well written in the Vajiram package.

Welfare schemes for vulnerable sections of the population by the Center and States, and the performance of these schemes; mechanisms, laws, institutions, and bodies constituted for the protection and betterment of these vulnerable sections.		This is a vast issue of social justice and has to be structured in order to grasp it in detail in a logical manner. It has been made into a table-type learning structure, which an aspirant has to fill time and again whenever relevant facts related to this topic emerge.
Issues relating to development and management of the Social Sector/ Services relating to Health, Education, and Human Resources.	The quality of higher education in India requires major improvements to make it internationally competitive. Do you think that the entry of foreign educational institutions would help improve the quality of higher and technical education in the country? Discuss. The public health system has limitations in providing universal health coverage. Do you think that the private sector could help in bridging the gap? What other viable alternatives would you suggest? ... 10% weightage	This topic is common between human geography and economics. A multi-dimensional analysis of 2 sectors – education and health – covering all; primary, secondary, and tertiary sub-sectors, is required. The questions are anticipatory in nature, and they can be answered once the basic minimum knowledge exists. For this topic, there is no clear-cut source. An aspirant has to take inputs from segregated copies of newspaper analysis.
Issues relating to poverty and hunger.	Though there have been several different estimates of poverty in India, all indicate a reduction in poverty levels over time.	Poverty, hunger, and malnutrition are again multi-dimensional topics with diverse sectorial linkages. The issue is

	Do you agree? Critically examine with reference to urban and rural poverty indicators. ..... 5% weightage	related to social, economic, geographic, and environmental factors too. However, an aspirant is advised to study at least the concept of the poverty line, hidden hunger, malnutrition, etc.
Important aspects of governance, transparency, and accountability, e-governance applications, models, successes, limitations, and potential; citizens' charters, transparency, and accountability, and institutional and other measures.	In the light of the Satyam Scandal (2009), discuss the changes brought in corporate governance to ensure transparency and accountability. "If the amendment bill to the Whistleblowers Act, 2011, tabled in Parliament, is passed, there may be no one left to protect." Critically evaluate. ..... 10% weightage	It is one of the most repetitive and overlapping sections. Coaching material may create a lot of confusion. Thus, an aspirant is advised to study related topics in yojna, especially special issues of e-governance and information communication technology.
Role of civil services in a democracy, India.		A common topic found in paper 4 of GS as well. It will be addressed there, taking into account the ethics of civil services and their role in democracy.
India and its neighborhood – relations. Bilateral, regional, and global groupings and agreements involving India and/or affecting India's interests. Effect of policies and politics of developed and	Project 'Mausam' is considered a unique foreign policy initiative of the Indian Government to improve relationships with its neighbors. Does the project have a strategic dimension? Discuss. Terrorist activities and mutual distrust have clouded India-Pakistan relations. To what extent could the use of	Although the weightage of IR has decreased this year to 20% from last year's 25%, it is still a significant part of paper 2 of GS. IR is an organic topic, yet it is scoring because of the limitation of the number of questions that can be framed in a year's development. One should start by reading the basic tenets of India's foreign

developing countries on India's interests, Indian diaspora. Important international institutions, agencies, and their structure, mandate.	soft power, such as sports and cultural exchanges, help generate goodwill between the 2 countries? Discuss with suitable examples. The increasing interest of India in Africa has its pros and cons. Critically examine. Discuss the impediments India is facing in its pursuit of a permanent seat in the UN Security Council. … 20% weightage.	policy, well elaborated in V.P. Dutt's 'India's foreign policy since independence' and the NCERT textbook of class XII 'Contemporary world politics.' For the current related scenario, there can be 2 methodologies – first, for continuous IR sections in newspapers, one should make entries into a separate diary dedicated to this task, and second, an aspirant may entirely leave IR for the last month before mains to be read from Vajiram's dedicated book on IR. Another book titled 'Contemporary international issues and affairs' by Swati Mahajan is a substitute for the Vajiram package. An aspirant should read either one of them but not both.

Comments On GS Paper 2 Of CSE (Mains):

The syllabus of paper 2 may look enormous, but an organized study can considerably reduce efforts. The whole part of international relations can be done in less than one week. Why? Look at the questions of IR in paper 2. None of the questions talks about the intricacies of strategic deals, terms of bilateral economic treaties, or terms of cultural exchange programs with visa requirements fluctuating now and then. Thus, this factor must be taken into account while maintaining the diary of IR. If that part is done religiously and astutely, the aspirant may not even require any coaching notes at the end of the day. Further, V.P Dutt's book is like a novel – it should be read just for the sake of curiosity – when the aspirant is mentally tired due to any reason. The same holds true for the NCERT of political science. It talks of the world situation during the Cold War and after that the formation of international bodies, their roles, mandates, etc., and would be called for again in the economics of paper 3.

The problem of welfare schemes for vulnerable sections will be troublesome. These need to be structured into the following table.

Discussions on	Women	child	SC/ST	OBC	Disabled	old	Street vendors
Constitutional provisions.							
Legislation – acts and bills.							
Recent judgments							
Government schemes.							
National policies							

The aspirant is encouraged to fill the table themselves. This would be beneficial not only for the GS part but also play an important role in the essay.

Governance is yet another aspect that may lead to confusion due to repetition. This aspect would also be found to a large extent in GS paper 4. An aspirant is encouraged to think along the following lines and extract material pertaining to it and develop it in the form of notes;

a) What is good governance?

b) What are the ethics underlying good governance?

c) Mechanisms to promote it – RTI, Citizens' charter, Transparency pact, ICT, and e-gov.

d) Suggested reforms in bureaucracy.

e) Recent legislations that promote good governance, such as the whistleblowers act, lokpal, lokayukta, etc.

◈ GS PAPER 3: Technology, Economic Development, Biodiversity, Environment, Security and Disaster Management

This is the most organic paper of general studies. The underlying principles remain the same, but the current development changes every year. These static principles, such as those of economics, science and technology, environment, and biodiversity, are utmost needed at the level of preliminary exam. An aspirant appearing for the mains examination is expected to build upon these principles and reflect on the current issues related to the above subjects.

Moreover, the topics in this paper will find most relevance while writing an essay. This paper has a clear-cut 3 areas – science & technology, economics, environment/ecology. The topic of security and disaster management was newly incorporated in the changed syllabus of CSE 2013. It is a highly dynamic topic which deals with both internal and external security of India as well as cyber security – a fallout of technological revolution during the last decade. Disaster management finds its presence in the explicit syllabus after the whole country had witnessed the devastating effects of flash floods in Uttarakhand in 2012. It has become a subject of grave importance as one realizes that human life is fragile in the present-day overexploited world by anthropogenic activities.

Because of the dynamic nature of the subject, an aspirant shall not find himself/herself limited to only textbooks, but a lot of current inputs would be required. Here again, those diaries of segregated information and analysis of newspapers would play an important role. Remember, my dear aspirants, that this paper can take a toll on your preparations if you just try to gulp down the facts because their numbers would run into hundreds. Thus, picking and choosing information and then its multi-dimensional analysis is the mantra for this paper. Also, the topics in this paper can't be seen in isolation from each other. Thus, it may happen that a person may categorize a question to be more of economic in nature, while another may categorize the same question to be more of environmental in nature. For example, would there not be economic effects of a new innovation or invention in science and technology? Would there not be environmental effects of that same phenomenon? And can it not change the security structure of the country by diminishing or aggravating old or new threats? This approach has to be constantly followed while discussing this paper. But let us first analyze the GS paper 3 for the year 2015 so as to chalk out the focus areas.

Analysis of GS paper 3 of CSE (Mains) 2015:

Course content	Questions in CSE Mains 2015 and percentage weightage,	Additional readings (over and above preliminary preparations)
Indian Economy and issues relating to planning, mobilization of resources, growth, development, and employment.	The nature of economic growth in India is described as jobless growth. Do you agree with this view? Give arguments in favor of your answer. ... 5% weightage	The basic text that an aspirant must have read by now is the NCERT Class XI textbook. This needs to be supplemented by reading the first 3 chapters of Uma Kapila's 'Indian Economy Since Independence.'
Inclusive growth and issues arising from it.		Yojana issue with related headings can be read. Certain chapters of the 12th plan document will also be relevant.
Government Budgeting.	The craze for gold among Indians has led to a surge in the import of gold in recent years, putting pressure on the balance of payments and the external value of the rupee. In view of this, examine the merits of the Gold Monetization Scheme. ... 5% weightage	The basics of government budgeting are explained very well in the Class XII NCERT economics textbook of macroeconomics. The budget analysis of the latest year must be incorporated into the studies before the mains exam.

Major crops, cropping patterns in various parts of the country, different types of irrigation and irrigation systems, storage, transport, and marketing of agricultural produce, and issues and related constraints; e-technology in the aid of farmers.	How can the 'Digital India' program help farmers to improve farm productivity and income? What steps has the Government taken in this regards? ... 5% weightage	This topic is closely related to economic geography and a base for this has already been created by reading NCERT geography textbook of class VIII and X. APMC in its all respect must be known by now. An aspirant must watch out for any issue of kurukshetra particularly in this regard.
Issues related to direct and indirect farm subsidies and minimum support prices; Public Distribution System – objectives, functioning, limitations, revamping; issues of buffer stocks and food security; Technology missions; economics of animal-rearing.	In what way could replacement of price subsidy with Direct Benefit Transfer (DBT) change the scenario of subsidies in India? Discuss ... 5% weightage	These issues find only a slight mention in NCERTs, thus these have to be supplemented by reading Uma kapila. Two things are important – PDS; challenges and changing forms, and, India's stand in WTO regarding subsidies. These are also elaborated in Sriram package for economics.
Food processing and related industries in India: scope and significance, location, upstream and downstream requirements, and supply chain management.	Livestock rearing has a big potential for providing non-farm employment and income in rural areas. Discuss.	This topic also overlaps with economic geography. These days, look out for emerging business models of mobile applications and aggregator models like OLA and OYO.

	What are the impediments in marketing and supply chain management in the industry in India? Can e-commerce help in overcoming these bottlenecks? ... 10% weightage	
Land reforms in India	In view of the declining average size of land holdings in India, which has made agriculture non-viable for a majority of farmers, should contract farming and land leasing be promoted in agriculture? Critically evaluate the pros and cons. ... 5% weightage	Read the chapter on land reforms, its evolution, and current practices in Uma Kapila. Look out for recent legislation in Yojna.
Effects of liberalization on the economy, changes in industrial policy, and their effects on industrial growth.	"Success of 'Make in India' program depends on the success of 'Skill India' program and radical labor reforms," discuss with logical arguments. ... 5% weightage	The phenomenon of liberalization and its effect on trade, industry, fiscal, and financial structure has already been dealt with in NCERTs. Now, this would attract 2 types of questions – one related to the broad effect of liberalization on a particular sector and the other related to any specific bill, act, or amendment that relates to service or industrial sectors.
Infrastructure: Energy, Ports, Roads, Airports, Railways, etc.	There is a clear acknowledgment that Special Economic Zones (SEZs) are a tool of industrial development, manufacturing, and exports.	Infrastructure is a vast area. Divide it into 2 broad topics – economic and social infrastructure. The former consists of energy, public/ civil, transportation, and

	Recognizing this potential, the whole instrumentality of SEZs requires augmentation. Discuss the issues plaguing the success of SEZs with respect to taxation, governing laws, and administration. … 5% weightage	communication infrastructure. The latter consists of health and education sectors, which have been studied earlier.
Investment models.		Study here PPP, BOLT, BOOT, FDI, etc. One upcoming is PPPP. All this has to be segregated from internet resources regarding its arrangement, issues, and applications.
Science and Technology: developments and their applications, and effects in everyday life.	What are the areas of prohibitive labor that can be sustainably managed by robots? Discuss the initiatives that can propel research in premier research institutes for substantial and beneficial innovation. … 5% weightage	This has a total weightage of 15%, which is the same as that of last year. S&T of GS mains will be quite different from what is being asked in the preliminary examination. There are 2 ways to do this section. Either an aspirant must always be vigilant about the S&T section in the newspaper and write it in a separate dedicated notebook to be referred to later, or one can read the compiled version of S&T in Sriram's package and a book titled 'Contemporary Science and Technology' by Pranav Mahajan. In both cases, an aspirant is advised to be organized and structured; otherwise, a huge amount of data will cause pain. No historical evolutionary background of I.T., space,
Achievements of Indians in science and technology; indigenization of technology, and developing new technology.	What do you understand by 'Standard Positioning Systems' and 'Protection Positioning Systems' in the GPS era? Discuss the advantages India perceives from its ambitious IRNSS program, employing just 7 satellites. … 5% weightage	

Awareness in the fields of I.T., space, computers, robotics, nanotechnology, biotechnology, and issues relating to intellectual property rights.	India's Traditional Knowledge Digital Library (TKDL), which has a database containing formatted information on more than 2 million medicinal formulations, is proving a powerful weapon in the country's fight against erroneous patents. Discuss the pros and cons of making this database publicly available under open-source licensing. ... 5% weightage	computers, robotics, etc., is required. IPR must be focused on more than the rest.
Conservation, environmental pollution, and degradation, environmental impact assessment.	To what factors can the recent dramatic fall in equipment costs and tariff of solar energy be attributed? What implications does the trend have for the thermal power producers and the related industry? The Namami Gange and National Mission for Clean Ganga (NMCG) programs and the causes of mixed results from the previous schemes. What quantum leaps can help preserve the River Ganga better than incremental inputs? ... 10% weightage	Weightage of this part remains the same. Here, a revision of the 'teachers' handbook on environment' would be required, and the aspirant has to go through the whole book instead of part readings as suggested in the preliminary. The other suggested reading is of recent judgments of NGT and the Supreme Court in this regard.
Disaster and disaster management.	The frequency of earthquakes appears to have increased in the Indian sub-continent. However, India's preparedness for mitigating	The whole circular process of disaster management, along with basic definitions, will be found on the website of NDMA. If an aspirant is

	their impact has significant gaps. Discuss various aspects. … 5% weightage	reluctant to find information on the internet, then he/she may read a separate book on Environment and disaster management by Dr. B. Ramaswamy. There is a high possibility that a question may be based on any recent disaster which occurred or was averted. So please look out for that.
Linkages between development and the spread of extremism.	The persisting drives of the government for the development of large industries in backward areas have resulted in isolating the tribal population and the farmers who face multiple displacements, with Malkangiri and Naxalbari foci. Discuss the corrective strategies needed to win the left-wing extremism (LWE) doctrine-affected citizens back into the mainstream of social and economic growth. … 5% weightage	The weightage of this whole section remains the same at 25%. Thus, this topic has taken a visible priority from UPSC. These topics are important not only for GS but also for essays. An aspirant is required to prepare essays on cyber security, internal security, and social media. These are the most dynamic topics of all the course as there is no single source of information. An unorthodox way would be to hunt some bureaucrat linked to some security agency and seek his/her help. However, that option may not be available to many. Thus, to enlist materials, it is recommended to study Vajiram notes for this topic. The practice question paper of vision coaching for this part is also worth trying.
Role of external state and non-state actors in creating challenges to internal security.		
Challenges to internal security through communication	Religious indoctrination via digital media has resulted in Indian youth joining ISIS. What is ISIS and its mission?	

networks, the role of media and social networking sites in internal security challenges, basics of cyber security, money laundering, and its prevention.	How can ISIS be dangerous for the internal security of our country? Discuss the advantages and security implications of cloud hosting of servers vis-a-vis in-house machine-based hosting for government businesses. Considering the threats cyberspace poses for the country, India needs a "Digital Armed Force" to prevent crimes. Critically evaluate the National Cyber Security Policy, 2013, outlining the challenges perceived in its effective implementation. ... 15% weightage	
Security challenges and their management in border areas; linkages of organized crime with terrorism.	Human rights activists constantly highlight the view that the Armed Forces (Special Powers) Act, 1958 (AFSPA) is a draconian act leading to cases of human rights abuses by the security forces. What sections of AFSPA are opposed by the activists? Critically evaluate the requirement with reference to the view held by the apex court. ... 5% weightage	
Various security forces and agencies and their mandate.		

Comments On GS Paper 3 Of CSE (Mains):

This section is the trickiest as well as the most tempting of all the GS mains content. Just because of the single reason that the course in paper 3 is the most diversified in its essence and nature. Aspirants will find the basic text insufficient to answer the type of questions asked in the mains examination in this paper. Thus, they would require searching for study material which increases their vulnerability to commercialization of information. Infinite numbers of books are available in the book stores – online and offline, the majority of which would contain repetitive content but in different well-designed colors. There are consultancies which conduct market research to provide information to the publishing houses on which color combination would appeal the most to buyers! An aspirant has to safeguard against this tendency of running into numerous materials and buying them without purpose.

One of my friends invited me to his place at Rajendra Place, Delhi, when he came to know that I intended to start preparations for civil services in September 2012. He threw open his small, rented room, which consisted of one bed, one study table, and an infinite number of books that were strewn on the bed and on the floor. One could not stand inside his room without stepping on the books, notes, study material, or whatever lay on the floor!

"You know, I just wanted to tell you that the more you read, the greater your chances of success increase," he advised me, gesturing toward the chaotic condition of the room. "How should I proceed with economics? That is a subject I can relate to," I asked him, still not finding my way into the room.

"First, read all the NCERTs from 6th to 12th class. Then proceed to Ramesh Singh. After that comes Uma Kapila, A to Z reading, cover to cover," he emphasized and after the pause continued, "Economics is a diverse subject. The above readings will only create a base. After this, you have to read the full 12th year plan document and then the plan, economic survey, and India yearbook. To compile all these, we would finally read the notes of Sriram." I was stunned by the volume of the suggested readings when he showed me these books.

When I proceeded with my preparations of economics on 12th October 2012 and had purchased all these books, within 2 weeks into the studies, I realized the repetitive matter and unnecessary details composed more than 90% of the material. Thus, it is suggested to the aspirant that for civil services, India yearbook and the five-year plan (complete) are both not required. In the plan document (a plan document is different from the five-year plan), selected chapters of significance, which an aspirant will identify during the course of preparations, and the flagship schemes of the economic survey, will suffice for the purpose.

My score in this paper was 80 marks, and that friend of mine who had even read the microeconomics from NCERT class XI scored 37 marks in the same paper and could not find his name in the list of candidates selected for the interview. However, the aspirant is motivated and encouraged to aim for a score of 100 marks in paper 3 of general studies.

◈ GS PAPER 4: Ethics, Integrity and Aptitude

The general studies paper 4 was a game-changer in CSE 2013. Candidates have scored from 130 to even 30 in this paper. The range of marks in this paper itself gives the incentive for working in a smart manner so as to outdo other candidates. The paper on ethics in GS mains 2014 was more analytical than that in the previous year. The intent of introducing this paper in civil services by UPSC was to bring to the forefront the importance of personal and professional conduct of civil servants. UPSC has tried to convey a message by introducing this course on how the country's non-political executive should align their conduct while performing their duty and otherwise. An aspirant may not become ethical or moral, inculcate values and the spirit of public service by studying this new paper, but at least he/she will have an indication of what is the requirement expected of a public servant. This message has rightly percolated into the minds of all the aspirants throughout the country and struck a chord even with those informed men and women who may not be aspiring civil servants but are aware of the happenings in our country.

After applauding the decision of UPSC to introduce this new course on ethics as an entirely different paper, I come straight to business, that is, the strategy to maximize your score in this paper. Let us see what the UPSC Civil services notification has to say about this paper.

"This paper will include questions to test the candidates' attitude and approach to issues relating to integrity, probity in public life, and their problem-solving approach to various issues and conflicts faced by them in dealing with society. Questions may utilize the case study approach to determine these aspects."

Reading the above sentences makes 2 things clear: first, that there will be some theoretical questions and other situational questions; and second, the situational questions would be framed in a manner so as to elicit the basic trait of a candidate's personality and to check whether he/she is adept as a civil servant or not. With these facts in mind, we proceed forward with the analysis of this GS paper 4 in mains 2015.

Analysis of GS paper 4 of CSE (mains) 2015:

This is the division of the course into topics and sub-topics, which makes it easier to organize the study content in a form that can be easily retrieved from memory.

PAPER IV				
STATIC			DYNAMIC	
Ethics and human interface	**Attitude, aptitude, and foundational values for civil services. Emotional intelligence**	**Contribution of moral thinkers and philosophers**	**Public/civil service values and ethics in public administration, probity in governance.**	**Decision making, case studies**
Essence, determinants, and consequences of Ethics in human actions; dimensions of ethics; ethics in private and public relationships. Human Values – lessons from the lives and teachings of great leaders, reformers, and administrators; role of family, society, and educational institutions in inculcating values.	Attitude: content, structure, function; its influence and relation with thought and behavior; moral and political attitudes; social influence, and persuasion. Aptitude and foundational values for Civil Service: integrity, impartiality, and non-partisanship, objectivity, dedication to public service, empathy, tolerance, and compassion toward the weaker sections. Emotional intelligence: concepts and their utilities and application in administration and governance.		Public/Civil service values and Ethics in Public Administration: Status and problems; ethical concerns and dilemmas in government and private institutions; laws, rules, regulations, and conscience as sources of ethical guidance; accountability and ethical governance; strengthening of ethical and moral values in governance; ethical issues in international relations and funding; corporate governance. Probity in Governance: Concept of public service; Philosophical basis of governance and probity; Information sharing and transparency in government, Right to Information, Codes of Ethics, Codes of Conduct, Citizen's Charters, Work culture, Quality of service delivery, Utilization of public funds, challenges of corruption.	

Comments On GS Paper 4 Of CSE (Mains):

My experience of studying the course of paper 4 was not good, mainly due to the reason that the content is highly repetitive. The part which was new, such as Ethics and human interface, Attitude and Aptitude for civil services, felt very alien while reading with coaching study material and some textbooks also. There will be a tendency of being lost in the book. An aspirant may feel that, irrespective of a lot of reading in the above subject matter, he/she is not able to recall or correlate the readings. To counter such tendencies, one has to create notes – topic-wise notes – as mentioned in the notification. While doing this, an aspirant should eliminate the tendency to stray here and there. This will become clear in the example below;

While dealing with the first topic, the course is written along with it.

ETHICS AND HUMAN INTERFACE: Essence, determinants, and consequences of ethics in human actions; dimensions of ethics; ethics in private and public relationships.

Human Values – lessons from the lives and teachings of great leaders, reformers, and administrators; role of family, society, and educational institutions in inculcating values.

An aspirant must be precise in studying, creating notes, and then imbibing the following in his/her mind;

a)   What is ethics?

b)   What are the various dimensions of ethics?

c)   What are the determinants of ethics?

d)   Relationship between ethics, morals, and values.

e)   Relation between private and public ethics, along with examples.

f)   How are family, society, and educational institutes responsible for inculcating values in children?

g)   What values should they inculcate in them?

The list of above questions is not exhaustive, and the aspirant is encouraged to create more questions from the above-written content.

It is worth noting that the sentence in bold related to human values should be grouped under the heading of *"contributions of moral thinkers and philosophers from India and the world."*

Thus, it is more convenient to create questions out of the course and look out for the answers to these questions. This will certainly reduce or even eliminate the tendency to wander in the book or study material. The same exercise may be done for the *part "Attitude, Aptitude and foundational values for civil services, Emotional intelligence."* Aspirants are asked to create their questions and then look out for answers in the books and study material. The printed material of the institute Sriram is well-written in this regard.

Come to the part that deals with *"contributions of moral thinkers and philosophers from India and the world."* The candidate is asked to bring out the meaning of these statements by world-famous personalities in the present context. Thus, while studying this topic, an aspirant may not learn the exact teachings of numerous philosophers and personalities. Only the area of his/her work or contribution is sufficient to be known. Further, the term 'present context' is important and should not be ignored while elucidating the meaning of any statement. A current event, news, or phenomenon in connection to that statement will certainly create an impact. I will give you an example;

"There is enough on this earth for everyone's need, but for no one's greed." — *Mahatma Gandhi.*

This statement, in the current context, can be correlated to carbon credit trading, stalemate achieved in climate talks, crony capitalism, versus environmentalists, GDP-centered development, and so on.

Coming to the dynamic part of paper 4 of GS. Let us first discuss the topic *"Public/civil service values and ethics in public administration,*

Probity in governance." This topic is bound to find resemblance with the topic of good governance in paper 2. The role of civil services in democracy was, in fact, another topic in paper 2 that can be better dealt with here in paper 4 of GS. The best source of study for this part is the second administrative reforms commission report, which has touched every aspect of our country. In fact, some of the topics in this part are directly found in the report. Another important reading here is a book authored by Dr. B. Ramaswamy titled as 'Public/civil service values and ethics in public administration.'

The most important part in the whole of paper 4 is the decision-making on case studies. It carries around 50% of the weightage, and that signifies the intent of UPSC. Upon grilling the candidate in a myriad number of tough scenarios, it is highly probable that the true character of the candidate would lay bare in front of the examiner, who would then determine whether or not those characteristics are adept for a civil servant. Thus, an aspirant is to be very cautious in dealing with these situational decision-making questions.

The approach that I shall tell you about is based on an algorithm with a series of sequential steps that would indeed help you arrive at the appropriate conclusion. The basic tenets of the algorithm are given below;

a) In any situation, identify the stakeholders – they may not be natural persons but also juristic.

b) For any situation, many options are possible. Identify those 2 actions which create an ethical dilemma. (If the question has given all the possibilities, then there is no need for this step.)

c) Analyze all the probable possibilities of actions with the tools of standard concepts of utilitarian and teleological method. In the former, if benefit is served to the maximum number of people, then the chosen option is correct. On the other hand, the teleological approach takes into account whether the means to achieve the desired end are correct ethically or not.

d) There are 2 more approaches but rarely used. First is the justice approach, and the other is the right-based approach.

e) Apply the utilitarian and teleological approach for every option that is given in the question, and then come to certain conclusions.

f) Then an aspirant shall ask some golden questions to eliminate all but one option that would be the action taken in the given scenario.

g) Some of these golden questions are whether the benefit is in the long run or short run, what would happen if all the people follow a particular option or action, and whether any action compromises the dignity of women or the law of the land.

The above-said approach will become crystal clear once a sample question analysis is done. Further reading suggested is 'Ethics in governance: resolution of dilemmas with case studies' by Mohan Kanda.

Dear aspirant, paper 4 of GS is a high-scoring paper once you get your foothold in decision-making skills. Answers written in an organized fashion in this paper may fetch you even more than 100 marks, which will certainly boost your chances of selection.

❖ **Special section on Art and Culture:**

When we prepare for UPSC, especially the art and culture section, it is more important for the candidate to know what not to read than what to read, as a huge volume is present to boggle the minds of candidates. In other words, the section of art and culture suffers from the problem of surplus. In such a scenario, our focus should not divert to becoming the master of the subject but to maximize our marks. Indian heritage and culture is one of the important topics candidates cannot afford to miss. When viewed from 2 different angles, it simultaneously becomes the most difficult of all topics and, if approached in a structured manner, it is perceived to be a scoring section.

There is a general bona fide difficulty – that most of the aspirants are not from this subject background, so they find it difficult to cope with it. However, it is one of the scoring sections both in preliminary and mains if you get the right guidance and right material, and you know the exact depth and the extent to study. The importance of Indian Heritage and Culture is on a constant rise as far as marks devoted to this section are concerned from the year 2012 onwards. Another important aspect is that this section comes at the beginning of GS 1 Paper (around 20% weightage), which also means that a candidate who attempts this section well enough will carry that impression into further questions of GS paper 1.

The syllabus of Indian heritage and culture written in the notification of CSE reads like this. *'Indian heritage and culture, Indian culture, will cover the salient aspects of art forms, literature, and architecture from ancient to modern times.'*

Does this provide any idea of what exactly you have to study? NO. The aspirants then run through thousands of pages in the myriad study material that is present. In this, peer pressure governs the choices of study material rather than rationale. Thus, to make the life of an aspirant easier, we present here a brief of various topics which a candidate must prepare with full devotion for both mains and preliminary exams.

Basic backgrounds: It will be discussed in relation to religions like Buddhism, Jainism, and Hinduism, which will make the concepts clearer and will help study the art forms in an easier form.

Urban planning and culture of the Indus Valley Civilization, universities like Nalanda, Taxila, etc.

Dances and Music: Its origin, sources, classical forms, basic differences among the forms, and classification of the specific forms according to states.

Literature: Ancient literature such as Vedic, Buddhism, Jainism; Indian literature in science like Aryabhata, Sangam; medieval and modern literature; and regional literatures.

Architecture: IVC, Buddhist Architecture, Rock Cut Architecture, Architecture fundamentals, Temple architecture, different styles in Guptas, Rashtrakutas, Badami Chalukyas, Western Chalukyas, Rashtrakutas, Hoysalas, Pallavas, Cholas, Medieval Architecture like Indo-Islamic Architecture, Mughal Architecture, and modern architecture.

Paintings: Cave paintings, manuscripts, frescoes, murals, folk, modern, and contemporary need to be appreciated in relation to different styles, schools, and dynasties.

Sculptures: Basic understanding of terminologies like idol, image, icons, and iconography. Sculptures from primitive times from Harappa, Gandhara, and Mathura schools of art, Hindu idols, and sculptures from medieval, modern, and contemporary times.

Fairs and Festivals: Pilgrimages and festivals define the culture of India, with special reference to the diversity among the states.

Music: Origin, Development, main streams, basic concepts, Devotional music, Folk music.

Theater Cinema: The journey of traditional recitation of stories to the emergence of theaters in India, leading up to the modern concept of cinema and its development.

Art and Craft: Varied use of materials like wood, clay, ivory, glass, fabric, etc., and its quality of craftsmanship will be discussed.

Famous Personalities in Art and Culture: Distinguished personalities in paintings, architecture, cinema, theater such as Nek Chand, Satyajit Ray, Correo, and Pandit Bhimsen Joshi.

Cultural Institutions: These basically cover institutions from pre – to post-independence times, such as ASI, Asiatic Society, and Kala Bhawan.

Spread of Indian Art Culture to Foreign Lands: the influence of Indian art on South-East Asia, Sri Lanka, Burma, and Indonesia.

The above-mentioned are the explicit areas of study required for Indian heritage and culture as far as UPSC Civil services are concerned for both preliminary and mains. We request the aspirants not to divide the subject material for preliminary and mains examination as such. It is advised that, while studying for the preliminary exam, a candidate must give one reading to the above-mentioned topics and try to retain the maximum to the best of his/her capabilities. However, when the mains exam approaches, the facts and figures may get diluted, and at times the memory fails with regard to this section. But the aspirant should not be demoralized as the subject matter of study remains the same. One more reading of the same subject matter is sufficient to recall the blurring facts. Moreover, if 3 practice papers of repute are written by the candidate in a time-bound and space-bound manner, as is the current trend of CSE, this indeed will take the preparation and confidence to the zenith level.

Now the question is, what sources must be read to cover the aforesaid explicit course content. One of the better ways is to search for each of these terms on the internet and jot down basic points regarding that term. But this has to be done after reading some basic standard texts which are mentioned below. These will build a foundation of understanding Indian heritage and culture, over and above which additional knowledge can be acquired.

1.   Themes in Indian History, NCERT Class XII, Part 1, 2, 3

2.   Official Site of Culture and Heritage of India, www.indiaculture. nic.in

3. Ancient India, by Susan Huntington

4. Indian Paintings by B.N. Goswamy

5. Survey of Indian Sculptures, SK Saraswati

6. History and Culture of India by R.C. Majumdar

Preparations for the Personality Test

A delight it is to see your name among the list of successful candidates who are selected for the round of personality tests (PT) – that is what UPSC calls them – not interviews! This PT won't attract a bombarding of questions of general knowledge as seen in the game show 'kaun banega karorepati.' In fact, highly contrary to it, the board members would engage the candidate in a round of conversations and try to elicit the personality traits of that person and check whether these fall in line with the requirements of civil services. So what are those qualities which a civil servant must possess? Many of these must be very much evident to the aspirants as these have already been a part of discussions in paper 4 of GS. Some of these are honesty, perseverance, integrity, mental alertness, social cohesion, and leadership, balance of judgment, constructive approach, decision making, politeness, and many more.

Even though we know all these aspects, some of the aspirants score low marks in the interview, and others score very high. Nevertheless, the final selection takes into account both the score in PT as well as in mains. It may thus be possible that candidates scoring low marks in the interview may get through the final cut off if their marks in the mains examination are high. However, the importance of the interview in the present times can't be understated. The candidates selected for appearing in the personality test are placed quite neck-to-neck in this cut-throat competition, so this PT should not be taken lightly, especially when we have a wide range of marks awarded in the interview.

Therefore, our endeavor should be that an aspirant puts in genuine effort to do well in the PT. For this, some plain facts need to be understood. The contention that one should begin their preparation at least one month before the actual date of the interview is false. As we have discussed at the beginning of the book itself, Personality test preparation begins at the time when you decide to start studying for civil services. It is an ongoing process and not an immediate one.

Secondly, an aspirant must remember that the detailed application form presents you to the board before anything else. This has to be filled in with utmost care. It is suggested that the advice and help of selected candidates and teachers may be solicited for this purpose.

Thirdly, an aspirant has to be utmost cautious at the end of the interview. That would carry the last impression and might possibly determine your final score. This is from the personal experience of my own interview. At the end of the personality test of engineering services, after successfully answering most of the technical questions related to my subject, the chairman of the board changed the atmosphere from a serious one to one filled with humor. He asked me questions about my personal life, which I relished, and in the process became too casual in my approach. Instead of smiling, I was laughing out loud. I felt triumphant because I had answered most of the questions correctly, and I felt that the board members were delighted with my answers. When the score arrived, I found that the board had given me one of the lowest scores on the list!

In the CSE personality test, I was determined not to repeat this mistake. The whole interview revolved around my job profile, which I had already anticipated and was ready with balanced answers to opinion-based questions. Throughout the interview, I maintained my calm and controlled my delight as I had answered all the questions. At the end of the interview, a lady asked, while smiling, a factual question which I didn't know. I apologized for not knowing the fact with a smiling face. Till the last minute, I kept my posture balanced, only smiled but never laughed. The corrective efforts bore fruit when I found that I received 171 marks, which were about 10 to 15 marks above the average score.

GENERAL TRAPS, MYTHS, AND FREQUENTLY ASKED QUESTIONS

1) I have studied the developments of ancient and medieval India. It will be sufficient for art and culture in GS paper 1.

No. The reading of NCERTs, ancient and medieval India, forms the basis on which specific knowledge of art and culture has to be developed. For this, read the above section. However, do not think that specific knowledge can be built without knowing the socio-economic settings of the ancient and medieval world.

2) History is not just about memorizing facts.

A contention that is absolutely wrong. For prelims, nothing has to be memorized, and for mains, the suggested readings should be more analytical than factual. Please see the mains questions if this myth creates a hurdle in your preparations.

3) I read all news about politics and witness heated political debates on television, so as to be good in polity.

After the minor success at the preliminary examination of 2013, I was invited to a small party by one of my friends who had tasted that success 2 times earlier also. During the dinner, he switched on the debate on the TV channel Times Now hosted by Arnab Goswami. That was the first time I had witnessed such an outrageous debate live on a news channel. I inquired about the reason for my friend's enjoyment during the show. "These debates help you create an opinion, and these opinion-based questions would come in your mains examination in the polity paper."

My friend was a victim of the similarity created by 2 terms, polity and politics. Both are widely different. An aspirant is required to bring the polity out of the political news. For example, I may be least interested in what Mr. Kejriwal campaigns for, bringing the BJP govt to conduct elections in Delhi. But I have to check in the constitution that, as per A – 239AA, for how long can the president's rule stay in Delhi. What is the role of the Lt. Governor of Delhi in such a scenario when the capital is functioning with no elected government? Similar thoughts must baffle your mind while reading the political news.

As far as the debates on TV channels are considered, the more provocative a debate is, the higher its rating may be. Thus, it seems to me that there is a competition among the news channels and the hosts of the prominent shows to ask agitating questions on burning issues. The media is utterly callous to the intolerance that is being propagated by these methods of propaganda. Surprisingly, these shows are big hits. People are enjoying word wars – the murkier it gets, the more enjoyment it brings! Thus, dear aspirants, even if you have a little propensity for these prime-time political debates, please avoid them. They will do more harm than good, not only by wasting your precious time but also by making you an intolerant personality in the long run, which, in fact, is a character contrary to the quality of a civil servant.

4) How do I revise polity?

The better word should be how to revisit polity. Do it whenever you find suitable news which can have its root in polity. Imbibing polity is a continuous process. You can't just, one fine day, get up and take a pledge to remember all the articles by night. Even if you do so, it would be a redundant exercise. Remembering articles is not at all important, but their usage is.

5) The ethical decision-making questions in paper 4 can be answered without any preparation.

No, do not take that risk to write a layman's answers in that section. Use specific approaches in an organized fashion. This will only take your score to more than 100 plus. Also, these 125 marks would not require significant energies. I think practicing 6 or 7 questions in a time-bound manner and with space constraint is more than sufficient. Then why leave this stone unturned?

6) I don't believe myself to be an ethical person, so how can I score well in the ethics paper?

Your personal ethics won't play a major role if these are camouflaged in good preparation and organized structuring of answers in paper 4 of GS. However, during the course of study, you must try to align your personal ethics with the requirements of services; otherwise, there is a high possibility that it may be laid bare in the interview.

7) One should not bother about the compulsory language papers.

Dear aspirants, these compulsory papers are far from being innocuous. I have seen 3 candidates failing in either English or one of the languages that you need to take from those listed in schedule 8. It is even tormenting that if one fails in these compulsory language papers, he/she would not even receive marks in the other mains examination papers. Thus, you would simply not be able to know whether you have cleared the cut off for the mains or not.

Thus, it is a sincere advice that every aspirant must practice some previous years' papers of both the compulsory languages in a time-bound manner. This may be done a week before the mains examination. Also, in the actual papers, do not leave any section or even a question unanswered. I had practiced 3 Hindi papers of compulsory language which consisted of one essay at the beginning of the paper. But in the actual paper, there were 2 essays to be written in the 2013 mains. However, in mains 2014, again there was one essay to be written. The candidate is advised to practice writing 2 essays, which would require serious effort to complete the paper in 3 hours.

8) Marking in the civil services mains examination is random. High subjectivity is involved.

What you can't see is left open for umpteen interpretations. The marking procedure is not disclosed by UPSC, and the constitutional body has all the rights not to be under the ambit of RTI in paper setting and checking aspect, as upheld by the apex court. Thus, we must not debate and discuss these contentious issues. I advise aspirants to refrain from this debate at all forums and try to concentrate on their subject matter to enhance their chances of selection. All these unnecessary debates are unproductive and drain out energy from the body and mind. Please avoid these and concentrate on your target.

9) An aspirant should join a mock interview session.

Two or 3 mock interviews will definitely help an aspirant gain confidence, rectify mistakes, and, more importantly, interact with mature people of varied experience. In this regard, interview sessions held at Samkalp and Ramaswamy academies are close enough to simulate the actual interview experience.

10) Marks of the interview are totally based on the luck of the person that day.

In this regard, the author **Pranav Mahajan** of the book 'Deciphering the Personality Test' has compared the interview with a one-day cricket match. A batsman may be in form or out of form on that day. That is exactly what an aspirant must avoid. The fluctuations – the variations in the interview scores should be minimum. Stable behavior from your side is another part of the personality trait you must possess.

Nevertheless, there will be variations in assessment. To counter or minimize these variations, there was a proposal to conduct 3 or more interviews of the same candidate at different dates by different boards. The average of their scores shall be the marks awarded to that candidate. The change is still to be considered.

Yet, even in the present scenario, we must have faith in the intent and abilities of our constitutional bodies, such as UPSC. The system can't be biased or arbitrary, for it would have collapsed or altered drastically in such a scenario. Thus, it is a sincere advice to the aspirant to better focus on his/her character building rather than questioning the sanctity of our institutions.

11) People who are good-looking generally fetch more marks in the interview.

Not necessarily. But undoubtedly, people who are good-looking have an advantage of initial attention, which, if capitalized upon, can help secure those candidates good marks. Nevertheless, I have seen not-so-good-looking people scoring much higher than average marks by projecting and 'selling' some other more important personality traits needed for being a civil servant.

12) Female candidates generally get good marks in interviews.

It is written in the CSE notification that 'Government strives to have a workforce which reflects gender balance, and women candidates are encouraged to apply.' The statement can be subjected to multiple interpretations and extrapolated to any degree.

13) What are suggestible readings for an interview?

Pranav Mahajan has painstakingly deciphered the whole process of the personality test into smaller steps in chronological order in his book titled 'Deciphering Personality Test.' His eye for catching and reflecting upon minute details is impressive. Another is by Madhukar Kumar Bhagat titled 'How to Excel in Civil Services Interview,' which, along with general guidelines, contains sample interviews for a profound insight into what goes on inside the interview room.

14) What should we do if, at a continuous stretch of 4–5 questions, we don't have any answers?

There may be a scenario where the panel of experts enters into your weak domain and keeps on grilling you continuously for 4–5 questions to which you have no answers. In such a circumstance, 3 scenarios arise;

a) You keep on refusing that I don't know the answer, and with each refusal, pressure on the candidate to answer the next question increases. This may reflect in the body language, that is, sweating, shaking of legs, smiling out of humiliation, and embarrassment, etc.

b) You play a wild card and try to bluff the members. This is most dangerous as they would generally know the answer to the question they have asked. An example in this regard – one of the candidates had listed painting as a hobby. She was an amateur painter but not very aware of the technicalities of various forms of paintings. When asked in the interview what she generally painted, the reply was something like this, "Sir, I can paint not only Madhubani but also murals at times." The board may have sensed that she was self-boasting and signaled to a painting hung on the wall, "Is this Madhubani or what? Can you broadly classify the form?" She was now stuck and played the bluff, "Sir, this is Madhubani."

The board member again asked, "Are you sure?" But she had exhausted her options by now. "Yes, sir. Pretty sure."

The members won't tell on your face that you are trying to fool us. The marks awarded by them will reflect that!

c) Another option when you are stuck in an unknown area is trying to answer after seeking permission in words such as, "Sir/ madam, I don't have exact knowledge of the issue in question but I would like to share my perception about the same with your permission." Of course, the words that you select may change, but the effect and impression must be rightly conveyed.

15) I have a good command over language, thus I can write better essays.

A widespread feeling, especially among the freshers. But the contention is not true. Read the notification of CSE 2014 carefully. It says, "Credit will be given for effective and exact expression." Nowhere is it written that marks will be awarded for literary expression of an essay. Further, effective and exact language has to be simple, lucid, and terse. Dear aspirants, even I was suffering from the same myth when I started writing practice essays. Using difficult language, complex sentences may reflect, to some extent, my command of the English language. Nevertheless, it fetched me not so good marks because the content was less and hollow. Thus, more important it is to improve and enrich your content and to express that in a simple and uncomplicated manner.

16) One should begin with quotations.

On the contrary, quotations should be avoided at the beginning of the essay. They should be used in the body or in the conclusions, and only when you remember the exact words. You should never create your own quotes. For example, someone said, "............" or perhaps, an intellectual person once said, "..........."

17) Philosophical and general statement-type essays are easy to write.

Another myth. This thought is of an aspirant who has not yet found footing in various aspects of GS such as social issues, economics, environment, etc. The attraction toward philosophical essays is imminent because these will appear so true. Look at the philosophical essay of CSE (mains) 2013 – "Be the change you want to see in others" – Gandhiji. Repeat it in your mind and give it the slightest of thought. You will realize how true it is! The essay can be reversed into – How can you expect changes in other people unless you change first? Or maybe – If you want to change people, then set an example for them to emulate, and this can happen only when you change first.

Secondly, in the essay of CSE mains 2014, a statement is required to be elaborated: "Words are sharper than the two-edged sword." How accurate it seems. But just check the areas it is related to – an aspirant generally won't study much in these areas, that is, Communication and interpersonal skills as well as soft skills and diplomacy. An aspirant would find twinkle in his/her eyes upon deciphering the intent of the essay. But here is the catch. Try to write 500 words on it, and you will find succumbing to the essay. It would be difficult to generate ideas and may end up to a highly repetitive content in its essence, but differing only in language. Further, you shall find it difficult to support the philosophical contentions with diverse examples from current related events and persons. Thus, it is my sincere request to the aspirants that one should avoid these types of essay and focus on other areas.

18) Essays can only be dealt with using the knowledge of GS.

As we have discussed above, essays are nothing but a reflection of GS, so an aspirant would not require any additional new knowledge for writing essays, only what he/she has absorbed during the study of GS. However, to say that no practice of writing an essay is required would be completely false. An aspirant is advised to write at least 5 essays and get them checked by his/her teachers or experts in the field.

It must be noted that with the provision of an answer-cum-question booklet, the space for writing an essay is more or less restricted and needs to be assessed from the outset and while writing. Gone are the days when aspirants attached additional answer sheets to write elaborate essays.

Here, I must take the privilege to highlight the gross error one of my friends made in the essay of mains 2013. Disrespecting the fact that space is limited, he kept on writing, only to realize at the end that there is no more space left for a proper conclusion. Thus, the essay had to be ended abruptly. He was awarded 49 marks, and consequently, his name didn't reflect in the interview list. Therefore, in the contemporary times, an aspirant must write at least 5 essays, and that too in a space constraint similar to that of Civil Services Examination.

19) Engineering students have an edge over arts students.

I have generally witnessed arts students approaching me for help in preparations with dampened spirits, especially during this present CSAT controversy. My inference is that their contentions of relative disadvantage as compared to the engineering students work to their disadvantage further. Those aspirants from humanities background should not consider their self-worth any lower than any other engineering and management student. Take a look at the 'subject-wise analysis of GS paper 1.' You will find that there are subjects in GS where expertise level of more than class X is required, such as economics and geography for the preliminary examination. In addition to it, Polity and History would involve a detailed analysis when taken up in mains. On the contrary, science and technology will not, in any case, attract analysis at class XI and XII level and not even mathematical analysis up to the tenth level.

Thus, as far as GS is concerned, an arts or humanities student must act fearless. He/she is at a better footing than the rest of the competitors. This slight disadvantage for the arts students, apparently prevalent in paper 2 of CSAT, had been done away with by making it qualifying with a 33% requirement only.

20) You have to read a lot of current affairs from newspapers, magazines, and the internet to crack the preliminary examination.

Look at the previous 4 years' papers available on any platform. Upon cursory analysis, one may be able to tell that facts on current affairs are generally not asked. UPSC has refrained from stressing the memory of the aspirants. At most, what may be asked is the concept behind the current related news, especially in science and technology, and the environment.

Thus, when an aspirant creates segregated facts from newspaper analysis, underlying concepts should be more stressed upon. This habit, in fact, would be of much greater assistance in mains than in the preliminary stage.

21) Test series is mandatory to join.

For an aspirant who can create an exam-like temperament at home, complete the paper in a time-bound manner, and maintain honesty and integrity while taking the paper, a test series is not required to be joined in a coaching institute. In fact, you can always select mock papers from different coaching institutes so that a variety of questions with varied difficulty can be covered. Nevertheless, an exam-like setting can be created by enrolling in the test series program of that coaching institute whose papers appear closest to the pattern of questions asked in the actual exam. For this, an aspirant may seek the guidance of known selected candidates and their teachers who would provide an unbiased opinion.

22) I have successfully qualified preliminaries last year but could not get through mains. This year, it's better to focus on mains; preliminaries would be a cakewalk for me.

It is true that we must study everything with a perspective of mains examination in mind. This is well reflected from the 'Consolidated strategy for preliminary 2015' written above, wherein, for the first 9 or 10 months of preparations, a concrete foundation has to be created to build further concepts for the mains examination. You must realize here that the direction of study is mains-oriented. It is only in the last 2 months that full efforts are required to press the escalator to your specific requirements of cracking objective questions in the preliminary.

However, the contention that an aspirant who has successfully qualified the preliminary examination once would succeed every time in the same pattern of examination is highly misleading and even dangerous. To house this line of thought in mind is a treacherous trap.

One of my close friends said 2 months before prelims 2013, "You are a newcomer in this field. Do not neglect the preliminary examination. I know you study from a mains point of view, but do not neglect this first stage of the examination. So please join some test series or give a few papers at your home." I adhered to his genuine advice and started taking CSAT paper 1 and 2 at my home in a time-bound manner. I am indebted to his advice, but I regret the fact that the guidance he vouched for was not followed by him, and he could not clear the prelims cut off by a mere 10 marks. He had downplayed the fight in prelims 2013, or maybe clearing the prelims 2012 had made him complacent.

Any aspirant should not underestimate the competition in the preliminary examination. I would repeat here that I find the preliminary stage competitively tougher than mains, just because of the ratio of successful candidates. What an aspirant can do is to condense the last 2 months' preparation period to maybe one month, not less than that.

23) Can preliminary be managed while continuing a job in a PSU, government (center or state), bank, or private sector?

The question can be reframed as whether an aspirant can clear the preliminary without coaching while simultaneously engaged in some other pursuit. Undoubtedly, the task can be achieved. For this, discipline and dedication are required. If an aspirant adheres to the aforementioned chart/time table, the results can be achieved without coaching as well. I personally feel that an aspirant can manage 2 tasks in tandem, although the working hours will definitely increase. Furthermore, the last 2 months would be critical, and the aspirant will have to manage holidays during that period. If that can't be done, he/she may also resign from the present job for long-term goals.

Generally, it is only in the govt sector (center or state) that the atmosphere may be conducive for preparation, if the workload is less. In the present-day scenario, banks, PSUs, and private sector jobs are too demanding, which generally drains energy from an aspirant for any further course of concrete action.

24) Comment on the cut-offs in the preliminary examination.

Year, General, OBC, SC, ST, Ph1, Ph2, Ph3

2012, 209, 190, 185, 181, 160, 164, 111

2013, 241, 222, 207, 201, 199, 184, 163

% increase, 15.31, 16.84, 11.89, 11.05, 24.38, 12.19, 46.85

2014, 205, 204, 182, 174, 167, 113, 115.................Max. Marks 385

2015, 107, 100, 93, 85, Expected cut off out of 200 marks.

There is also a minimum mark to be scored: 30 for paper 1 and 70 for paper 2, irrespective of any category. In 2013, and in 2014, these minimum marks were 40 and 70 respectively. The mammoth increase in the cut-off in each category is possible for 2 reasons that exist together: firstly, the preliminary examination of 2013 was easier compared to that in 2012, and secondly, competition is increasing due to the growing number of candidates and pattern predictability.

The cut-off for CSAT 2014 went lower because of 2 reasons; firstly, the maximum marks were reduced from 400 to 385, and secondly, the questions, in particular the paper 2 mathematics section, were a little tougher than that of previous years' paper.

25) The probability of success in CSAT increases with subsequent attempts.

An indeed frivolous perception prevalent among some aspirants. As the role of subject in-depth knowledge reduces and that of managing your time during the examination increases, it does not matter whether it is your first attempt or second attempt, and so on. What matters the most is that, whatever attempt it may be, you must practice how to adjust and synchronize your effort in line with the current requirement of UPSC, reflected from its question-setting trends.

26) I could not solve a question during the practice test, but somehow I will manage it in the actual exam.

Take a scenario when an aspirant doing a test paper is not able to do a maths question within a time-bound condition. No worries. Try it after you are through with the paper. Still, if the aspirant is not able to do it, then he/she should immediately revert to the solution and understand the underlying concept. Because there will not be any miracle in the actual exam that you shall be able to do a similar question under the pressure situation.

In this regard, I will take up my own example. I find myself better in mathematics than in reading comprehension. But there seemed to be a problem when I used to do work and time questions. I was generally rendered frustrated by these questions whenever I encountered them in the practice tests of CSAT taken under a time-bound scenario. As a result, I had to leave them unattended. However, during the analysis of the paper, I was able to do such questions when there was no time constraint. I didn't take it lightly. I once got hold of around 50 such questions and solved them during one single sitting. The purpose was to build up speed and to chalk out my approach for these kinds of questions.

It would have been a grave error to think that I would somehow miraculously do such questions under extreme pressure of the actual

CSAT exam, in spite of the fact that these were a definite logjam in practice papers.

27) I couldn't clear CSAT 2014 because of paper 2 and just missed the cut off in paper 1 of CSAT 2015. Thus, I am thinking of dropping the attempt of CSAT 2016 and giving it in 2017 so that I can have sufficient time to increase my subject knowledge.

This is the worst you can do to your career. Try to understand the scenario. A candidate who has given preliminary 2014 must have been studying for at least one year. Unfortunately, he/she couldn't get through the preliminary for 2 consecutive times. Now the assertion is that if the person takes the exam in 2017 after a break in 2016, he/she will be rendered with 'sufficient' time for building the subject knowledge. That means for the attempt of 2017, he/she will have at least 4 years of time to build up that threshold level of knowledge. Think rationally, does the preparation require 4 years of study? What can't be done in 3 years of study won't be accomplished in the 4th year.

It is not the lack of time the candidate is suffering from. Thus, dropping the attempt of 2016 in the pursuit of the 2017 attempt is a sheer waste of time and bad planning.

General Advises & Pitfalls During the Preparations

◈ Prerequisites to Crack UPSC Civil Services

Please do not confuse this with the characteristics of a civil servant that have been discussed above in the section of the interview preparations. These are the mandatory characteristics/techniques a candidate must possess or cultivate to crack civil services.

a) **Patience:** the very first attempt would take at least 10 months of serious preparation until the mains examination. The interview will be held around 3 months after the mains examination. Then comes the anxious waiting of one month or so before the final results are displayed. During all this time, a candidate may take an occasional break but can't rest in peace. He/she must be in continuous touch with studies. Thus, this period of more than one year, and preferably 1.5 years for the very first attempt, has to be covered patiently. There will be moments when you feel that it's a lost battle, yet you have to keep your calm.

b) **Perseverance:** An aspirant has to continuously engage with books and other study material. Patience for 1.5 years will bear fruit, not without persevering efforts. I personally find that aspirants in this field do not lack patience – many have devoted their youth primarily to this task.

c) **Smart study:** without this, the combination of the above 2 will not bear fruit. This is what this book is all about. Unlike hard work, smart study focuses on picking and choosing targets and their timely fulfillment and taking immediate corrective action if required. We don't vouch that an aspirant has to study everything under the sun but study what the requirement of an exam is. Continuous monitoring of progress and rectification wherever needed is the need of the hour. We vouch for organized and structured study using charts, tables, and algorithms which shall definitely help a candidate imbibe a plethora of information and then reflect upon it.

Other aspects and virtues, such as hard work, determination, confidence, answer writing skills, strong oral communication, concentration, memory, etc., are indeed an added advantage. They can be cultivated and developed by an aspirant but directed under the broad umbrella of the 3 mentioned above; that is, patience, perseverance, and smart study.

◈ What Do the Candidates Lack in General?

Although all the above-mentioned aspects are required for success at civil services, out of the 3 listed above, patience is the most common aspect found in many candidates. Perseverance is found in some, and the skill of smart study is quite rare.

One senior person whom I met to discuss history before my mains examination candidly said, "I came to Delhi from Bihar in 2003 and now in 2013 I am again going to Bihar as I have cleared Bihar state services." He took a pause. "It pains me to find that I devoted my youth to UPSC Civil services and still could not crack it." He didn't lack patience. In fact he had an excess of patience!

A very close friend of mine who hails from Bihar guided me thoroughly in regards to what I should study when I started the preparations. He is a hardworking guy who can stretch upto 12 hours a day of self-study and that too for more than a week without any break. Unfortunately he didn't clear prelims. Further, there is absolutely no doubt in my mind in regards to his knowledge for almost anything. His efforts were persevering and conduct was patient but he lacked a strategy of smart study.

This book is dedicated to all the aspirants like him who can do miracles if pushed slightly in the right direction. All that is required to be done is to channelize their immense potential in the required direction.

◈ Calculating the Number of Hours of Study

There are many situations which throw upon an aspirant the illusion that he/she is studying but in fact that is not study at all. One person I met in 2012 when I was yet to take the decision of going in for the preparation said, "My dear friend. First think and then decide whether to go for preparations or not. Because you have to study at least 12 hours each day and every single day throughout the period of 2 years." I got scared as I perfectly knew that with the best of my efforts I could not study for more than 5 or 6 hours each day. He continued, "You will have at least 8 hours of coaching each day, then in the peer group you must discuss what is taught in the class for around 2 hours and then before retiring to the bed you must take out another 2 hours."

After clearing the examination I realized that this accounts for only 2 hours of study. The time devoted to coaching must not be counted in your study hours. The time you spend discussing and debating with your friends, whether the issue is relevant or not, should not be included in the study hours. The number of hours you study is the self-study you do sitting alone in your room. And that, if around 6 hours average each day, is more than sufficient to crack civil services in first attempt.

◈ Role of Calendar

Use calendars with enlarged fonts of dates and place it in such a place where it is easily visible. Its role becomes prominent 2 months before prelims and 2 months before mains. For each day that passes place a cross with black pen on that date and write what progress you made in your studies. For the coming day list your target, which in fact, should put an inflationary pressure on you. For each day you do not take to study cancel the date with a red pen. This would put an aspirant under pressure and his/her performance would set on an increasing trend.

◈ Countering Fatigue

An aspirant must not think himself/herself to be a machine. We are human beings and we get tired. It is not only our right but also our duty to refresh our debilitated energies periodically through the means of leisure activity. After 5 days of continuous slogging and burning midnight's oil for civil services, you may feel restless the sixth day. This restlessness can be countered if you periodically take breaks from study after 6 pm on the sixth day. The time till you sleep on that day must be spent in your way – that should not include studies or even the discussions of studies. The ways of relaxation may be different but all should bear the same output – that on the very next day you feel rejuvenated when you get up in the morning – ready again for the same slog till the next break.

◈ Mobile Phone Anxiety

We must accept the fact that all the present aspirants and the future ones have been a witness to the technological revolution in India, especially during the last one decade, in varying degrees. The accessibility, availability and affordability of mobile phones have led to its penetration spanning almost the whole country. Its usage is frequent and the number of average hours spent on mobile is on a rise. With its integration with internet in smart phones, the PC/laptop traffic is diverting on mobiles. This has led to a syndrome of mobile phone anxiety. Try to live without a mobile phone for a single day and you may witness the same. But my dear aspirant, this syndrome has to be countered when exams approach. Let us say one month before preliminary and 2 months before mains one should avoid the usage of mobiles. The unavoidable usage should be at your convenience and not on others' wishes.

One girl whom I had always known as a hardworking aspirant had her mobile switched off for continuous 5 days one month before preliminary 2014. She called me up on the sixth day only to make me realize that apart from being a hardworking woman she had also become smart enough to manage her time when she said, "Because I am studying for civil services my time is a priority now rather than yours as you have achieved the goal. So, I will call you whenever I require your assistance or I feel like talking to you and you are supposed to respond to my calls! If you call and my mobile is off do not panic, I am consumed in my prayers!"

I liked her approach to deal with the exam-time pressure and successfully counter the mobile phone anxieties.

◈ Coaching – Studying V/s Socializing

An aspirant joins a coaching institute with great fervor to pursue his/her target. But I have seen and heard many cases of that enthusiasm becoming perverted to some other pursuits. We must realize that our goal stands above all. But it is disheartening to see quite few cases of broken love stories emanating from some prominent coaching institutes. I admit that socialization for a human being is a natural process and in fact necessary for the survival of human as a species. However, if that process leads to broken hearts and consumes your energies for a purpose so ineffective and even contradictory to your solemn goal then it must be stopped.

In fact, the scenario is such that people join coaching institute 'to forge out a relationship if nothing happens.' This statement came from a girl whom I knew quite well. Her prime motive had become perverted during the mis-directed path of preparations. Same scenario with a slightly different intent exists with the guys. These tendencies are meant to be curbed by the aspirants themselves, proliferate better thoughts among their peers and even the teachers and faculties of institutes must be a little more vigilant and percolate this message to future leaders of the country.

◈ Theory of Compartmentalization

This theory is used in the context of World War II when America dropped the atom bomb on Japan to bring it to an immediate end. How did America develop that atom bomb in utmost secrecy that was required for the success of the mission? It was done by the methodology of compartmentalization. The various departments and its numerous arms working on the project knew only the details relevant to that particular department. Nobody expects the president and his close comrades knew the full scope of the project. When everybody knew partial information, the probability of information leakage was reduced drastically, and the mission was executed successfully.

The same methodology may be used in a different sense and an entirely different context. While an aspirant is studying for UPSC Civil services, he/she is encouraged to carve out compartments in the mind dedicated for a special task only. For example, when a person is studying, he/she must not think about his/her relationship. When taking a break on the 5th or the 6th day as per the convenience and the requirement of time, an aspirant must not think of studies. This segregation of the thinking process is required to be done so as to input a chunk of energies into the required task. A vivid example of this is one of the most respected men of our country – the metro man – Mr. Sreedharan. When asked how he managed to achieve such a colossal task in an overcrowded place such as Delhi, he replied that while in his office he did work and nothing else, and that too in a disciplined fashion during the office timing only. After the office time, he never took any work home and gave full time to his family.

◈ The Photoelectric Effect

Some metals, when bombarded with photons of a minimum characteristic energy, release the electrons from that metal, which then constitute a current. If you bombard that metal with any number of photons at a speed below the critical energy requirement, nothing will happen.

Cracking the Civil Services Examination finds similarity with the law of nature. There is a minimum energy you have to spend to crack civil services in any one attempt. For example, if 100 units are required to get into the list in any one year, then an aspirant dissipating 25 units for 4 years won't get the result. You have to put in a minimum critical effort in any year to get through the civil services. Then why shouldn't it be the first attempt!

Epilogue

With the above discussions, I end on a delighted note the contents of this book. It is expected that aspirants of civil services benefit from these discussions by translating the words into action. The aspirants, as well as the concerned society, may also be enlightened by the lop-sided study pattern delivered in the big coaching institutes for just fulfilling their monetary ambitions at the cost of innocent aspirants and their parents. I really hope that the coaching industry gets into a mode of self-realization and corrects its program structures and related costs so as to do more good rather than harm to the society.

The aspirants must realize that self-study is the prerequisite for success at Civil Services Examination. The future builders of the nation are required to be self-motivated rather than spoon-fed by the traditions of rote learning. They are required to always remain in a 'mission mode,' task-oriented approach, the foundation of which is incepted when we start our preparations and is carried into the services.

Furthermore, I encourage all readers to think and deliberate upon the issues listed in this book, in order to engage in a wider debate regarding the same at various forums. Any suggestions and criticisms are most welcome and will be incorporated into the text of the book.

www.ingramcontent.com/pod-product-compliance
Lightning Source LLC
Chambersburg PA
CBHW040756120726
48005CB00012B/1197